VINTAGE
LIVING
TEXTS

THE ESSENTIAL
GUIDE TO
CONTEMPORARY
LITERATURE

A. S. Byatt

SERIES EDITORS
Jonathan Noakes
and
Margaret Reynolds
with Gillian Alban

D1081010

Also available in Vintage Living Texts

American Fiction

Martin Amis

Margaret Atwood

Louis de Bernières

Roddy Doyle

Sebastian Faulks

John Fowles

Susan Hill

Ian McEwan

Toni Morrison

Iris Murdoch

Salman Rushdie

Jeanette Winterson

'An excellent and timely series, very useful for students, well-produced and well-written.'
Dr Robert Eaglestone, Royal Holloway,
University of London

'I am impressed. Students will find these texts extremely useful, and serious general readers, too.'
Professor Chris Woodhead, former Chief Inspector of Schools

'Margaret Reynolds and Jonathan Noakes are at the cutting edge of providing English teachers with the support they need for teaching the contemporary novel.'
Dr Vivian Anthony, Training Co-ordinator, Professional Development Services for HMC schools

'Two highly sensitive and intelligent teachers (from school and university) lead us into dialogue with the author, the texts and their context and help us to question what and how we are reading and to arrive at illuminating answers. Such dialogue is the essence of good practice in teaching literature.'
John Venning, Head of English,
St Paul's School for Boys, London

'This series is the first to teach students what they most need to learn: how to teach themselves. It is informative, rigorous and yet, more importantly, playful. It combines the qualities of the best teaching.'
Anthea Church, Head of English, Kent College, Pembury

'I didn't realise just how good the series was until I started working closely with it. The questions are so thoughtful and probing, and the analysis provided allows the students to lift their own understanding. The texts really do occupy their own niche between guides purely for teachers and the ubiquitous student crib, and are much better than either.'
Michael Parker, Head of English, Newington College, NSW, Australia

'This is a terrific series. The text and the reader's response are at the heart of these guides; the tone is authoritative but never dogmatic, while the style is enthusiastic and approachable. The series is aptly named – not only are the subjects still alive, so too are the guides.'
Lucy Webster, *The English Magazine*

'*Vintage Living Texts* are very modern. They are certainly democratic as they give the literary text to the reader, prompting personal critical response without suggesting what those responses should be. They will be a blessing to teachers and students.'
Iain Finlayson, *The Times* Play Magazine

'These guides, designed to reflect the National Curriculum, are likely to appeal also to university students, and those who take their reading group seriously.'
Independent Magazine

'In addition to sixth formers and undergraduates, the series also works well for those taking the International Baccalaureate or on EFL courses.'
Liz Thomson, *Publishing News*

VINTAGE
LIVING
TEXTS

A. S. Byatt

THE ESSENTIAL GUIDE
TO CONTEMPORARY
LITERATURE

Possession: A Romance
Angels & Insects
A Whistling Woman

VINTAGE

Published by Vintage 2004

2 4 6 8 10 9 7 5 3 1

Copyright © Jonathan Noakes and Margaret Reynolds 2003

The right of Jonathan Noakes and Margaret Reynolds to be identified
as the authors of this work has been asserted by them in accordance with
the Copyright, Designs and Patents Act, 1988.

First published in Great Britain in 2004 by Vintage
Random House, 20 Vauxhall Bridge Road,
London SW1V 2SA

Random House Australia (Pty) Limited
20 Alfred Street, Milsons Point, Sydney,
New South Wales 2061, Australia

Random House New Zealand Limited
18 Poland Road, Glenfield,
Auckland 10, New Zealand

Random House (Pty) Limited
Endulini, 5A Jubilee Road, Parktown 2193, South Africa

The Random House Group Limited Reg. No. 954009
www.randomhouse.co.uk

A CIP catalogue record for this book is available from the British Library

ISBN 0 099 45221 9

Papers used by Random House are natural, recyclable products made
from wood grown in sustainable forests; the manufacturing processes
conform to the environmental regulations of the country of origin.

Typeset by Palimpsest Book Production Limited, Polmont, Stirlingshire

Printed and bound in Great Britain by
Bookmarque Ltd, Croydon, Surrey

While every effort has been made to obtain permission from owners of
copyright material reproduced herein, the publishers would like to apologise
for any omissions and will be pleased to incorporate missing acknowledgements
in any future editions.

CONTENTS

A Whistling Woman

VINTAGE LIVING TEXTS:
REFERENCE

Acknowledgements

We owe grateful thanks to all at Random House. Most of all our debt is to Rachel Cugnoni and her team at Vintage – especially to Ali Reynolds – Jason Arthur, Liz Foley, Katherine Fry and Jack Murphy who have given us generous and unfailing support. Thanks also to Caroline Michel, Marcella Edwards, Philippa Brewster and Georgina Capel, Michael Meredith, Angela Leighton, Harriet Marland, to all our colleagues and friends, and to our partners and families. We would also like to thank the teachers and students at schools and colleges around the country who have taken part in our trialling process, and who have responded so readily and warmly to our requests for advice. And finally, our grateful thanks to A. S. Byatt for her work without whom . . . without which . . .

VINTAGE
LIVING
TEXTS

Preface

About this series

Vintage Living Texts: The Essential Guide to Contemporary Literature is a new concept in reading guides. Our aim is to provide readers of all kinds with an intelligent and accessible introduction to key works of contemporary literature. Each guide suggests techniques for reading important contemporary novels, and offers a variety of back-up materials that will give you ways into the text – without ever telling you what to think.

Content

All the books reproduce an extensive interview with the author, conducted exclusively for this series. This is not to say that we believe that the author's word is law. Of course it isn't. Once his or her book has gone out into the world he or she becomes simply yet another – if singularly competent – reader. This series recognises that an author's contribution may be valuable, and intriguing, but it puts the reader in control.

Every title in the series is author-focused and covers at

least three of their novels, along with relevant biographical, bibliographical, contextual and comparative material.

How to use this series

In the reading activities that make up the core of each book you will see that you are asked to do two things. One comes from the text; that is, we suggest what you should focus on, whether it's a theme, the language or the narrative method. The other concentrates on your own response. We want you to think about how you are reading and what skills you are bringing to bear in doing that reading. So this part is very much about you, the reader.

The point is that there are many ways of responding to a text. You could concentrate on the methods you might use to compare this text with others. In that case, look for the sections headed 'Compare'. Or you might want to do something more individual, and analyse how you are reacting to a text and what it means to you, in which case, pick out the approaches labelled 'Imagine' or 'Ask Yourself'.

Of course, it may well be that you are reading these texts for an examination. In that case you will have to go for the more traditional methods of literary criticism and look for the responses that tell you to 'Discuss' or 'Analyse'. Whichever level you (or your students) are at, you will find that there is something here for everyone. However, we're not suggesting that you stick solely to the approaches we offer, or that you tackle all of the exercises laid out here. Choose whatever most interests you, or whatever best suits your purposes.

Who are these books for?

Students will find that these guides are like a good teacher. They introduce the life and work of the author, set each novel in its context, explain key ideas and literary critical terms as they arise, suggest comparative exercises in a number of media, and ask focused questions to encourage a well-informed, analytical approach to reading the novels in a way that is rigorous, but still entertaining.

Teachers will find in this series a rich source of ideas for teaching contemporary novels and their contexts, particularly at AS, A and undergraduate levels. The exercises on each text have been tailored to meet the various assessment objectives laid down in the subject criteria for GCE AS and GCE A Level and the International Baccalaureate in English Literature, and are explained in such a way that they can easily be selected and fitted into a lesson plan. Given the diversity of ways in which the awarding bodies have devised their specifications to meet these assessment objectives, a wide range of exercises is offered. We've had fun devising the plans, and we hope they'll be fun for you when you come to teach and learn with them.

And if you are neither a teacher nor a student of contemporary literature, but someone reading for your own pleasure? Well, if you've ever wanted someone to introduce you to a novelist's work in a way that will let you trust your own judgement and read more confidently, then this guide is also for you.

Whoever you are, we hope that you will enjoy using these books and that they will send you back to the novels to find new pleasures.

All page references to *Possession: A Romance*, *Angels & Insects* and *A Whistling Woman* in this text refer to the Vintage editions.

A. S. Byatt

Introduction

In an essay entitled 'Fathers' published in *On Histories and Stories* in 2000, A. S. Byatt says: 'My own short novel, *The Biographer's Tale*, is about these riddling links between autobiography, biography, fact and fiction (and lies).'

It is an interesting remark: A. S. Byatt casts herself as a writer of fiction ('My own short novel'), who sets conundrums, sifts for treasure and puzzles us with wordplay ('riddling'); who makes connections ('links'); who exploits different forms and genres ('autobiography, biography, fact and fiction'); and who teases us with the possibility that none of this is true ('(and lies)').

At the beginning of the interview included in this book, Byatt starts on an explanation about her ideas of 'romance' by saying 'My mind is naturally inclusive'. As a voracious reader, an eminent academic, and a philosopher and critic, Byatt's work gives us access to an astonishing breadth of reference and systems of thought. Nothing is too large for her, and nothing too small. But everything is connected and inclusive. One idea will always lead on to another as nothing comes to her singly. Which is probably why she has always been compelled to write fiction.

Byatt has experimented with other forms of discussion within her fiction. In *A Whistling Woman* Frederica Potter becomes the host on a new and inventive television show called *Through the Looking Glass*. This is an arts discussion programme like no other. A theme is chosen, eminent cultural critics are invited, art objects are portrayed or books discussed, images flicker across the screen to suggest, to hint, or provoke ideas beyond the actual topics under discussion. It is a brilliant notion. Yet it is a notion that can only work in fiction, and in Byatt's fiction in particular.

It works for two reasons. One concerns Byatt as a writer and the other refers to Byatt as a reader. As Byatt has a huge range of reference at her command, she is always willing to let one reference slide into another, and she is capable of describing the 'inclusiveness' of her imagined television series. On the other hand, Byatt herself is a reader and knows the pleasure of reading works in a doubled fashion. Byatt – or you, the reader – reads the text (in this case both the text of *A Whistling Woman*, and the included narrative of the fictional television programme) and continues to make yet more connections. We might wish that *Through the Looking Glass* really was available on our screens, but the truth is that the programme can only be so 'inclusive' and impressive because it is fictional.

Byatt has spent some of her working life as an academic teaching English literature at a university. In 1983 she became a full-time writer and she says, in a personal statement offered on her official website, that 'I held a full-time university teaching post for eleven years and now feel entirely happy, for the first time in my life, at the prospect of writing full time, thinking things out from beginning to end, and reading for my own purposes'. As an academic, Byatt's many professional skills included ordering, seeking, shaping, collecting, analysing, cataloguing, listing, sorting and filing. You can see that these processes still intrigue her and she uses them imaginatively and often in her fiction: for example, in the cataloguing and sorting undertaken by William and Matty in her novella 'Morpho Eugenia', or in the research quest through libraries and collections undertaken by Maud and Roland in her novel *Possession*. But, for Byatt, that sorting is not an end in itself; it's the linking that she focuses on. This playful linking, a 'riddling linking' may, in fact, be precisely the opposite of the neat academic ordering which she describes so well.

Byatt has often said that scholarship and formal paths of knowledge – fact – can only take us so far. There will always be things that are unknown, things that are hidden and which can only ever be imagined. This is why she added the 'Postscript' to *Possession* as she says in the interview:

> The narrator tells the reader what happened in the
> Postscript. Nobody in the modern time knows that.
> And I think this is partly me saying 'Look . . . with
> scholarship, you think you will get to the end of the
> quest and find out what this person was really like,
> and what they really felt, and actually the chances
> are that the most important moment of their life, or
> most important moments, are forever hidden'. So it
> was partly a theoretical matter of principle to tell
> people things that couldn't be found out by scholars.
> In that sense I was also saying a novel is better than
> a biography, or that a novel does things a biography
> can't do.

If imaginative connections and inventive links are part of Byatt's key qualities as a novelist, another is her love of language. The 'riddling' pun in the quotation from her essay on 'Fathers' has been pointed out, but glance at virtually any page of Byatt's work and you will see how she exploits the possibilities of wordplay with a verve and an abandon that is distinctive. It's in the very title of *Angels & Insects*, where one story turns on the near-anagram of insects/incest. It's in *A Whistling Woman* where Frederica, pregnant, is 'full of life'. Above all, it's in *Possession* where wordplay on the word 'Ash' is exactly one of the open, known things that help Roland and Maud to learn the punning clues to the unknown, hidden story of Christabel LaMotte and Randolph Henry Ash.

It's not just a pleasurable game. A careful analysis of why puns and wordplay work shows how this is actually connected to the pleasures of reading and understanding. In the interview included in this guide Byatt says:

> That's what I so love about metaphor. I've got a
> theory about metaphor now. That we take such
> pleasure in it because it's where the synapses cross
> and two sets of association become, briefly, the same,
> and for some reason this excites us immensely. Like
> we're excited by visual images where we can't work
> out whether its an old woman or a young woman.
> All the ones that Wittgenstein got excited about. Is it
> a vase or is it two faces? We like anything that's on
> that kind of ambiguous edge.

When Byatt says 'we' here, that is exactly what she means. As a dedicated reader herself, Byatt writes movingly about the excitements of reading – especially in *Possession*. But she is conscious also that she can communicate the same pleasure to her own readers.

> It felt as though I was trying to hold everything
> together, and the other was always shimmering
> underneath. And I wrote all the poems thinking,
> none of these poems should exist without having a
> clue towards the modern story, as well as existing in

the past as part of the story. So there is a lot of this kind of verbal flickering, which is, of course, at its very root – it's the nature of reading. That's why we read in a scholarly way, that's why we read critically, in order to hear the flickering of the words, both then, and now.

'Then and now' always count for Byatt. In *Possession*, the 'then' of the Victorian story is carefully set against the 'now' of the present story. In the quartet of novels which includes *The Virgin in the Garden*, *Babel Tower*, *Still Life* and *A Whistling Woman*, Byatt does something even more curiously complicated with 'then and now'. The stories in each have a chronological line spanning from 1953 to 1980. But you have to work hard to realise that they end as late as 1980, because the final novel, *A Whistling Woman*, ends in 1968, and it's only in the second novel, *Still Life*, that you find that the Prologue goes beyond the ending of the fourth and last novel because it is set in 1980. If that sounds complicated, then it is, but it does have a purpose.

In another essay, 'Old Tales, New Forms' in *On Histories and Stories*, Byatt says, 'I stumbled, whilst working, across the idea that stories and tales, unlike novels, were intimately to do with death.' Byatt goes on – in her 'inclusive' way – to refer to Scheherazade, to the drowning man who sees his life pass before his eyes, to Boccaccio's *Decameron*, and Marcel Proust's *A la recherche du temps perdu*. One of her arguments is that children love stories because they see themselves existing in an 'infinite' time where there is no death. Older people love stories because they know that they exist in a 'finite' time and that will come to an end with their own death. In between are the worries about 'motives and responsibilities' that take up the urgencies of middle age.

It's a persuasive argument. It makes us realise that all of Byatt's fiction – stories and novels – are about death, and a defence against death. Time – as in her quartet of novels or even in *Possession* – has no relevance, because it weaves in and out and around, and resists shaping, sorting, ordering, cataloguing, listing. Byatt's imagination 'includes' everything and isn't limited by finite boundaries.

It is this same principle that is at work in the allusive, referential style that is Byatt's distinctive trademark. With her use of form (or antithesis of form) one idea will always lead on to another, one word will always translate into another, and no story will ever come to an end.

Interview with A. S. Byatt

London: 2 April 2003

JN: *Possession* has the subtitle, 'A Romance'. What versions of romance you are playing with in the novel?

ASB: My mind is naturally inclusive and once I'd had the idea, I decided to include every conceivable version of romance. But it did start with Nathaniel Hawthorne who defined a romance as 'a novel that didn't have to keep strictly to the truth and could include elements of fantasy', and I also think Hawthorne was talking about the historical novel as being a kind of imaginative structure as opposed to the realistic account. So I started with him, and then I thought, what other meanings are there: and I thought of medieval courtly love, and I thought it's a love story both in the past and in the present, and then I thought about Tennyson reworking the Arthurian legends.

And then, I think quite late on in the planning of *Possession*, I got it into my head that I should also be parodying modern romantic literature in some sense; it should be, as it were, a modern love story. So I was writing a parody of Georgette Heyer. There are one or two scenes in it that are pure – in my mind – scenes out of Heyer that I read and read when I was little. So it's all those things, working together.

JN: Is there also the romance of the archive and of a kind of romantic quest of scholarly endeavour?

ASB: Yes. The moment I saw that there were going to be two scholars was the moment I realised that there could be two romances, a modern one and an old one. Of course, any kind of archival work is a kind of detective story, so I wound a Margery Allingham quest into it. But there is also the sense of the Holy Grail, the knights riding out into the forest to find the hidden object. So it was very much about all these things.

JN: You say that your mind is inclusive, and I can see the way in which your title, *Possession*, is used in a very inclusive way as well. Could you explain about the kinds of possession that you were tackling in the novel?

ASB: I think this is the only novel I've written in which the title word is the first thing I've thought of. The story I like to tell – which is a true story – is how I used to watch Kathleen Coburn, the great Coleridge editor, walking round and round the circular catalogue in the British Museum library and I thought, 'Here is a woman who, as far as I can see, spends every waking moment, and a lot of the sleeping moments, of every day, thinking about Coleridge.' And then the word came into my mind, with the immediate sense of demonic possession. I thought, 'Does he possess her? Has this dead man taken over this living woman?, or has she taken possession of him, because we read his thoughts as mediated by her?' In some ways, the manner in which she has arranged his thoughts in the Notebooks, according to a system entirely of her own, is faintly irritating, because you have to read his thoughts in the order in which she has put them, rather than reading Notebook by Notebook. Then I discovered, from talking to Coleridge scholars, that she had actually, rather secretly, carried away a lot of his Notebooks to Canada, and had only – from the mid-Atlantic – telegraphed the Coleridge scholars in England saying, 'Notebooks on their way to Toronto, perfectly safe, will be well looked after.'

That gave the idea of economic and financial possession. Of course, Henry James plays with the word 'possession' – 'great possessions in great houses' – owning *things*, and I realised that actual manuscripts are things which people fight for the possession of. I wrote in a newspaper in 1970: 'I think of writing a novel called "Possession",' and I didn't publish it till 1990, so there was a long gestation. About five years after I'd thought of the title, I thought of the sexual meaning of the word 'possession', and I thought if it was looking for something, something like the Browning love letters, then you could have modern lovers looking for ancient lovers, and you would have a sort of plot that would almost make itself – which it did.

JN: And which of the two plots – the nineteenth-century plot, or the twentieth-century plot – came to you first?

ASB: It came as it is – very much in the order it is in the book. It's a quest, and I went on the quest, and I found the objects. One of the most difficult things was, in fact, to delay the discovery of bits of the nineteenth-century plot, unnaturally, really – because once you have found all the correspondence, what is there left to find? So I had to invent all the bit about Christabel having gone to Brittany, in order for there to be more plot. So then I thought, well, why would she have gone to Brittany? And then I thought up the baby, and then I saw that this was a romance of a quite beautiful kind. But an enormous amount of the plot was invented in order to keep the process of discovery going. I was never, to be truthful, as interested in the modern plot, except as a detective story. Or in the modern people's emotions. When they made the film, I think they assumed – because they were Hollywood Americans – that the story is a story about the young modern lovers, whereas actually, almost all *readers* know that the story is an occluded story about the Victorian lovers, and the other two are there for finding it out.

JN: The reader is also turned into a detective. You say that you delay the revelations, so the reader is left to pick up clues. Am I right in thinking that sometimes the correspondences are really quite minor? There is a moment in which Roland says to Maud that she has 'inherited Christabel's books' and I misread it as that she had inherited her 'looks'. I wondered if that kind of connection – a sort of verbal echo – is also woven in consciously?

ASB: It probably was. It felt as though I was trying to hold everything together, and the other was always shimmering underneath. And I wrote all the poems thinking, none of these poems should exist without having a clue towards the modern story, as well as existing in the past as part of the story. So there is a lot of this kind of verbal flickering, which is, of course, at its very root – it's the nature of reading. That's why we read in a scholarly way, that's why we read critically, in order to hear the flickering of the words, both then, and now. That's what we do it for. That's why we bother to read with care, rather than doing what the French call simply 'consuming'.

JN: There are also clues which are more obvious, such as the colour-coding.

ASB: Ah yes. I always colour-code my novels, it's not peculiar to this one. Christabel goes with green because of the green of the serpent woman and the Lamia and the Ondine and the water. And people get quite annoyed by it and keep writing to me, saying, 'Why is she green?', and I say, 'But fairies are always green.' I knew that when I read ballads when I was a little girl. The Fairy Queen appears to Tam Lin in green, and they go into a green hill. And then, of course, I was playing with the Victorian idea of the innocent blonde woman, the blonde woman as the good woman, and the dark woman as the bad woman. What else is colour-coded?

JN: There are frequent references to blondness and to whiteness, but also to goldness – golden hair – Wolff's hair for instance.

ASB: Yes . . . the whiteness goes with Blanche. And Blanche goes with Blanche Glover, and Blanche of course is beautifully invisible because you don't get a description of her face. The first time you meet her is in a poem by Christabel about white gloves being folded up and put away tidily, and the white linen, and the innocence and the clarity of it, and then there's the white milk which drips everywhere in one of Christabel's poems after the child is born. The golden hair was sort of seeing how far I could push the symbolic golden hair I had read about as a child and which George Eliot uses without even thinking. George Eliot's Gwendolyn [in *Daniel Deronda*] is in many ways behind Christabel. Gwendolyn has golden hair and resembles a snake and is always twisting her neck about like a snake. And then there's an extraordinary poem by Browning ['Gold Hair at Pornic'] about a buried woman whose golden hair comes tumbling out of the tomb when it opens up and in the hair are massive quantities of money which she's also hidden away because she's a miser, so you get gold coming out.

JN: And then the association of the colour blue with water and with various feminine images in the novel.

ASB: It's a novel that I always felt was really painted in primary colours. It was painted in very flat unnuanced primary colours. It was a bit heraldic. One of the original sources of it, of course, was Tennyson's poem 'The Lady of Shalott' where the Lady is sitting in the dark in the tower, working in the mirror, and putting all the beautiful colour of the outside world into the web that she is weaving . . . and she sees things flashing red . . . Sir Lancelot flashes red as he goes past . . .

JN: The names are woven into this as well, aren't they? So the idea of LaMotte, which suggests 'a moat', or the idea of 'bailey' being a guardian of the tower also fit in, in a playful way, to this whole notion of a literary heritage?

ASB: Yes. There is something quite astounding there. I am interested in real accidents. I thought of the idea of a motte and bailey castle because I thought of Christabel thinking of herself as an impenetrable fortress. She's a virgin lady who lives by herself, and she can't be got at, like the Lady of Shalott in her tower. Christabel is allowed to be a woman writer as long as she doesn't allow anyone to come into the defences of the motte and bailey castle. But the thing I hadn't known was that the story of Undine, the water serpent without a soul who loses her life when she marries a human man, was written by LaMotté Fouque. I just didn't know that. And of course anybody might think I had been terribly clever, whereas in fact I think the language was just playing games with me. You keep finding things like that and they make your hair stand on end. The motte and bailey was enough anyway, you see. I mean, I know I did it for that reason. I called Maud 'Maud Bailey' and put her as the descendant of these people who lived in this castle which was a sort of Victorian castle like the one that was built by the Tennyson d'Eyncourts when Tennyson's family became ennobled and built this huge thing which they couldn't keep up and which is now a ruin. That would do. I knew motte and bailey from my school history lessons as a ten-year-old, it was engrained in me. Whereas I don't know that I'd even known that the story of Undine had an author, until I started looking for it. And then it took me a lot longer to realise it was actually written in German, although the name of the author is French. It's all very exciting. Then when I read it, it all just fitted into the whole book.

JN: I had the impression when I was reading *Possession* that you must have enjoyed writing the pastiches. Am I right?

ASB: Yes. I was also very frightened. I didn't mean to do it. My first idea of the book was as a kind of palimpsest or veil. It was going to be the images on the veil – the critical writings, the modern writings – through which my readers would guess that the shapes of the things that were hidden behind the markings were not the same as the markings. So it was going to be that kind of very literary detective story. And then I realised as I went on that I was actually trying, as university teacher and as writer, to say that poetry is more real than criticism. Poetry does more things at any given moment than any critical account of it. It is not a historical object. It isn't a theory, it is a *thing*.

And then it struck me that since I had got so many layers of writing in this book, really it required there to be poetry in it that was *more than* the criticism. And then I felt really stuck for several weeks. And I bumped into [the poet] Dennis Enright . . . Oh and then I read a book by Robertson Davies in which he used some poems by Thomas Lovell Beddoes, an obscure Victorian poet, for the libretto of an opera that his characters were singing. He didn't say it was Beddoes but I happen to know because I'd had a passion for Beddoes at Cambridge. And I thought, 'I could do something like that . . . I could find a very obscure Victorian poet . . .'

But Dennis Enright said, 'Go away, Antonia, and write them yourself.' So I went home and started to see if I could. I wrote a little Christabel poem, sort of Emily Dickinsonish, and it *worked*. And I thought, 'OK, I'll try a bit of Tennysonian blank verse.' That worked. Then I thought, 'All right, I'll put them in.' Then they just wouldn't stop happening. They were part of a level of the texture of the piece I was writing that was absolutely essential. And I could do it, which I really hadn't thought I would be able to. Nobody has yet, that I know of, found an anachronism.

C. K. Stead, the New Zealand poet, wrote to me and said that he'd found an anachronism. He said, 'You've put the word "tricksy" in and that's modern'. And I said, 'No it isn't. It's out of [Shakespeare's] *The Tempest*. Prospero says to Ariel, ". . . my tricksy spirit . . .".' And he said two of the lines didn't scan – but they were both out of [Milton's] *Paradise Lost*.

JN: The pastiches also seem to me to be one of the ways in which you adopt many voices, and enjoy adopting many voices.

ASB: That was a very, very important time in my writing as a whole. I grew up as a novelist in a world where I felt there were a very restricted number of possible voices, and I felt they were more restrictive than they were. I felt that women wrote personal novels about people's feelings, and that you had to nuance people's feelings, and [novelist and critic] Angus Wilson was saying that you had to understand everything about people's motives. And I was actually bored to death by both of those things. I was actually interested in language. Being able to write in as many styles as this, for perfectly good and real reasons, was a tremendous release from feeling that you ought to write like Kingsley Amis, or John Braine, or somebody like that whose prose felt to me plonking and dreadfully limited. And I came to respect George Eliot who could write with many voices.

JN: Some of your characters also try to write with different voices. Sometimes characters act almost as ventriloquists for the voices of others. Even down to small details. I recall in one of the letters from Christabel that Ash complains that she is no longer speaking in her own voice, she's now adopted the voice of another. This seems, in other words, not just something you enjoy doing yourself, but something that has found its way, as a theme, into your novels.

ASB: I think this is true, and again, it goes back to the fact that this is a tremendously solid novel about the processes of reading and writing. Because any writer, when reading, starts a kind of ghostly parody – can I do this kind of sentence? You have to be careful what you read, when you're writing. And most novelists will tell you that they don't read novels when they're writing one. They read other kinds of writing – they want to keep their own voice. But equally, of course, there are times when you're just reading voraciously, when all these voices become part of you – they work in your head, they sing in your mind. I grew up on Victorian poetry as my mother gave me Victorian poetry as a very small child – I had a Tennyson book and a Browning book and I knew 'The Lady of Shalott' by heart and the 'Morte d'Arthur' by heart. Those voices were always in my head. But they never were able to get out any more, because I was meant to be talking like Elizabeth Bowen. That's one level. There is another level, which is that the great influence on all my generation was T. S. Eliot, and he cut voices together in *The Waste Land* and you felt, if you couldn't do that, you didn't know your craft. In fact, I suppose that most of the things I cared about were poetry, and all the things I wrote about were fiction, so there was something coming together there.

JN: Can I ask you about the 'Postscript'? First of all, about why you put it in?

ASB: I got into more and more of a panic as I approached the end because it became clear to me that, as the story began with Roland, so it ought actually to end with Ash – not with Roland. And I wanted the past to be more alive in the present than the present. That was one thing. And another was, I knew I had cheated my hero, which was Randolph Henry Ash, because he was a good man and a clever man, and had he not really gone on looking until he found out whether he had a child or not, he wouldn't have actually been the man I invented. If I had made a plot which allowed him simply to accept either that Christabel had killed the child, which clearly she had not – and when he thought about it when he went home, he would know she hadn't – or, that it was impossible for him to find the child, it wouldn't have worked. So, I thought, 'I will put this in.' And I am always seduced by putting *Paradise Lost* into the end of anything – so I put him into a summer garden where all the flowers were improbably flowering at the same time, whereas they would have in fact flowered sequentially.

There are three or four places in *Possession* where the narrator talks to the reader, and tells the reader things, the most important things, which the modern people in the novel never find out. The narrator tells the reader what Ellen Ash feels. The narrator tells the reader what happened in the Postscript. Nobody in the modern time knows that. And I think this is partly me saying 'Look . . . with scholarship, you think you will get to the end of the quest and find out what this person was really like, and what they really felt, and actually the chances are that the most important moment of their life, or most important moments, are forever hidden.' So it was partly a theoretical matter of principle to tell people things that couldn't be found out by scholars. In that sense I was also saying a novel is better than a biography, or that a novel does things a biography can't do. The beauty of a biography is its ghostliness.

20

I am just reading a biography of Ford Madox Ford, and the biographer doesn't know at what point Ford went to bed with his third mistress after he had decided to abandon his second mistress, and the mystery interests me as a novelist. Because of course, as a novelist, I could describe exactly how and when he went to bed with her, and that brings us on to the fact and fiction things one later started writing. But *Possession* is a proper novel. Those are proper novel moments. I occasionally get letters from people saying, 'You shouldn't have done that, you broke your convention.' I broke it — absolutely deliberately — for good reasons.

JN: The fact and fiction thing is also foregrounded at quite a few stages. There's one moment in *Possession* where a distinction is made between 'hard fact' and 'the passion and colour' which people can put on hard fact. Does that serve as an analogy for what the novelist does? Plunders history, and literary history, for raw material, but then transforms it, in their own mind, with colour and passion?

ASB: Yes, and you have to be very, very careful. I've been reading a lot about historical novels recently, and I think there are rules. I think it's very, very hard to write a good historical novel with a major person at the centre about whom a lot is really known. I had a long correspondence with a man in Dallas about whether a novel could have been written with Virginia Woolf as the central character. And I haven't read the one that was written and filmed recently [Michael Cunningham's *The Hours*, partly based on a reworking of Woolf's *Mrs Dalloway*]. My own feeling is that it couldn't work. I think there is so much surplus imagination invested by Virginia Woolf in Virginia Woolf, that if you put her in a novel, you make her smaller and thinner. Whereas, in fact, what you want is a peripheral person, if a real person at all, or a peripheral moment in a real person's life, in which you can insert brightness and colour.

I once wrote a whole short story because I got angry about a footnote in the letters of Robert Browning, in which he said that he couldn't go somewhere because the person he was going to visit had a guest who fell off a cliff while sketching. I got into a dreadful rage. I thought, 'Here's this whole person whose life was finished in a moment and all we are told, in a footnote, is that it interrupted Browning's travelling arrangements . . .' So I thought, well, I'd better not find out any more about this person, I will just invent the person. So I did a whole structure round it – it's called 'Precipice Encurled'. I then discovered that the person who fell off the cliff was a woman, whereas I had made mine into a man. It's that kind of relation between fact and fiction that is very profitable, I think. Whereas writing a novel about Princess Diana or Napoleon . . . you could only make pop art.

JN: The idea of metamorphosis is crucial in *Angels & Insects* – the notion of metamorphosis both as a classical allusion, but also as the idea of the butterfly metamorphosing.

ASB: Yes. I've always been obsessed by butterflies because they are so much more of a metamorphosis than any of the ones in Ovid. You get an egg, and then you get a grub, and then you get a chrysalis and then you get the creature. And they are very nice to look at because they are one of the easiest examples in which to see evidence of Darwinian changes, evidence of species changes as adaptation. And in the period when my novel is set, which is the year in which *On the Origin of Species* came out, you had these – I find very moving – young British naturalists on the Amazon, Wallace and Bates. I liked them because they weren't English gentlemen (they were English men from the shop-owning classes, but not the labouring classes that I come from myself), and they went out there out of sheer intellectual curiosity, not because they were gentlemen going on an adventure, and they discovered endless things. They sat on the Amazon for years and years, and Bates did actually work out quite a lot of Darwin's theory about the mutation of species.

One of the things I wanted to do with *Angels & Insects* was to make the aristocratic English people in the gentlemen's country house into an almost solidified morph, a thing that was not terribly capable of change, and the young man comes in all dark and full of life, and nearly gets trapped in it, like a spider's web. And 'morpho', also *morpho Eugenia* the butterfly – *morpho* means 'beautiful' in that sense – the butterfly morph form of the thing is at its most incredibly beautiful. But there's a historical allegory in there too, because they're all called the Alabasters, who are set like white statues, mostly called Anglo-Saxon names – like Sir Walter Scott's Anglo-Saxons in *Ivanhoe* – and William, the hero, is a sort of William the Conqueror. What he takes away is the cousin called Matty, who appears to be just called Matty, but is actually Matilda, who was the consort of William the Conqueror, which makes them the invading Vikings. So it's about theories of changes of society, in a jokey way, going back to Sir Walter Scott, whom I love, but nobody ever reads now.

JN: I realise now that much of the imagery is used in the moment when William comes home and finds Eugenia with Edgar – she is actually metamorphosing through all those processes.

ASB: I thought about how he could leave when he had all those children (I write these novels about good men and then end up having to work out how they could be so stupid), and I actually thought up the idea of the incest in order to explain why he didn't feel any obligation to the children: he thinks of them as little white grubs, white babies he thinks appear to have nothing to do with him. It's a quite different form of whiteness from the whiteness that's in *Possession*. What it absolutely isn't is racially determined, although the Anglo-Saxons go with the whiteness.

JN: Thinking for a moment about the incest and the word-play with which you connect 'incest' and 'insects': this sort of wordplay is important in your novels, isn't it?

ASB: Yes. And yet when I was young I'd always assumed that it was one of the things I simply couldn't do. I can't do crosswords, for instance. I am a person who cannot solve a crossword. I can't understand it, it bores me even; people give me a clue and I think, what's the point of trying to work it out? It's more that wordplay happens when a book I'm writing is really working, and all the language I have in my head is sort of fusing together. And it just came to me in a flash. I thought of the incest before I thought of the pun, because it seemed to me that British county families are reasonably incestuous anyway. They have a very small circle of people they can marry and from the point of view of Darwinian breeding theory they are very inbred. So that all worked and this was just the extreme version of being inbred and I thought it was very funny. But the wordplay just came because my mind was scanning and scanning and noticed. And then I remembered that there was this wonderful moment in [Jane Austen's] *Emma* when they play this word game with the tiles, and Mr Churchill pushes a word across to Jane Fairfax and really upsets her, and I thought, you could do that, because they all played this kind of word game constantly of an evening. All that just came to me as though I'd discovered it. It happens when I'm writing very fast, it's like changing key in the middle of a piece of music.

That's what I so love about metaphor. I've got a theory about metaphor now. That we take such pleasure in it because it's where the synapses cross and two sets of association become, briefly, the same, and for some reason this excites us immensely. Like we're excited by visual images that we can't work out, whether it's an old woman or a young woman. All the ones that Wittgenstein got excited about. Is it a vase or is it two faces? We like anything on that kind of ambiguous edge. And insect/incest – it doesn't mean very much, but for some reason it's peculiarly delightful in the word field of this book.

JN: Something else that strikes me very strongly about your style, is that you like to build through rhythms. For instance, you build the phrase 'because he loved her' and you play on different varieties of the word 'love', 'beloved' for example [pp. 46–7]. Does that kind of effect also come to you in the same way in that the anagram 'insect/incest' came to you, or is it something that you work on in a conscious way?

ASB: No, it feels musical, but it comes to me. Again, it only comes to me if I've got what I refer to as the whole word field of the work I'm working in. I mean, there are certain rhythms you can't use in certain works because they're out of other works, or they're too modern or whatever. And this, in a way, is a certain rhythm of a scientist, trying to think scientifically. 'He knew, because he loved her, that she was blinded by tears, and he guessed, because he had studied her, because he loved her, that her pride would be hurt if she thought her tears had been seen.' And that's both mimicking his thought process and me explaining, half an inch behind him, how he got to that thought process. But it is mimetic in both cases. It shows both my thought process and his inner rhythm. 'Nor could he say, "I love you: I want to comfort you because I love you".'

It's also, in fact, in *Possession* – Roland and Maud say to each other they don't use the word 'love' any more, and I think love is a very, very difficult word to put in a modern novel, although of course in a Victorian novel it has to be very, very prominent. So it's playing with that as well – the distance between a modern novel and one of the past. I found when I wrote my book of essays that young male British novelists have a deep nostalgia for romantic love, whereas the women don't at all. If you read the novels of Julian Barnes and Ian McEwan, the heroes are desperate to re-establish a context in which romantic love has meaning. I think the women have completely given up, and in a sense the people who really feel love in my novels are, on the whole, men!

JN: That's very interesting!

ASB: It *is* interesting . . . I don't understand it, but it's interesting.

JN: There is also – going back to *Possession* for a moment – a discussion at one point between the way in which the Victorians understood romance *in toto*, the whole concept of romance, whereas now we have a vastly proliferated vocabulary about sexuality and love, but we no longer understand the concept of romance.

ASB: I think that's very true. When I wrote *Possession* – partly because I was only recently out of the university – one of the things that was obsessing me was the neo-Freudian, neo-Lacanian discussion of sexuality *ad infinitum*, and the sexual analysis of every sentence, the gender analysis of every sentence of every book, of every poem. I felt that that really was a 'murdering to dissect', that the essence – not only of love, but of sexuality – was going with all this vocabulary being put upon it. And Roland and Maud look at each other rather ruefully and say 'we talk so much that we can't feel'.

I did feel that with some of my students. That they were

so hyperconscious of their sexuality and hypothetical terms, that it must have been quite difficult for them to respond, in an ordinary way, to a person. Indeed, I went to talk to a group of psychoanalysts last week and one of them said to me, 'We just have no vocabulary for talking about wanting somebody.' I found that very moving.

But I'm now bothered by the other end of it, which is the popular culture end of it. I'm bothered by people getting up on the television and discussing their feelings, laying their souls bare – you know, my brother's boyfriend's mother's father tried to seduce my sister's aunt, and now we're all going to come on the stage and hit each other. I can't stand all this. I was talking to a psychoanalyst about this and she said, 'Confession is repression', and she's dead right. One of the things that I feel about the Victorians in both of these Victorian novels is that they had very rigorous rules about what they should and should not do – which meant that if they broke them, it was a real act of violence.

We have so few rules that there is almost nothing that we should not do – which almost means that there is nothing that is really interesting to do. Equally, the Victorians also had a set of references with heaven and hell and good and evil and right and wrong, within which they could place their behaviour, not with reference to their own wants or needs – as to whether they were too fat or too thin or whether it would be good for them to have a relationship with this person or whether it might be better for them to be in a relationship (which is a phrase I hate) with some other person of a more suitable kind. They had to think seriously. They made themselves very miserable. And quite a lot of them killed themselves. I'm not saying that I would rather have lived then. I am very happy being a twenty-first-century woman, making my own choices.

JN: Is it useful, though, to think of you as a novelist – almost like a medium – who is interested in the communion of spirits from the past? It's an idea that comes into 'The Conjugial Angel' as well as into *Possession*.

ASB: Yes. Well, I think that, again, particularly reading poetry is to be haunted. One is haunted by the rhythms of the speech, and therefore of the thought of dead people. And the rhythms get into your blood and this is the way a ghost would get into your body. It is the way, of course, that your ancestors are in your body, they are actually moving around your body and your blood. Which is OK.

But it is partly thinking of Browning, who did refer to himself as a ventriloquist. Browning wrote a poem, just as an exercise, in almost every voice of almost every period, of almost every civilisation he'd ever even begun to think about. To be able to write somebody's rhythms is to be able to imagine them in a way in which to talk psychoanalytic and gender criticism about them is – in a way – *not* to be able to imagine them, but to distance them. Having said that, I wouldn't like to say that I believe I live in the past. I believe that both *Possession* and *Angels & Insects* are modern novels, written by a modern novelist, who is *not* trying to recreate the atmosphere of a Victorian novel, but only to hear the rhythms of one.

JN: And in any case, you're looking at them with the perspective of now – the playfulness especially makes that clear.

ASB: Yes, and the perspective of now comes in and is made clear. Because then you can hear the other – whereas if you simply write pastiche, you can't hear either.

JN: Thinking of your ancestors for a moment, I'm struck by your first epigraph to *A Whistling Woman*: 'A Whistling Woman and a Crowing Hen / Is neither good for God nor Men.' And you say this is a frequent saying of your maternal grandmother?

ASB: Yes, she used to say it in broad Yorkshire, and glare at you. She always said it like clockwork if I tried to whistle – and for all sorts of other things that you might try and do and that she thought were not feminine. She was a totally unfeminine person. She was a sort of large, short, shapeless object that simply sat in a chair, radiating ill will. And most of the things you did she enjoyed disapproving of, so it comes from there.

JN: And how have you used that expression, 'a whistling woman'?

ASB: I chose it as the title for the novel very early. It must have been in the 1960s. It was meant to be the last of my quartet. I had an idea that with any luck, the woman, or women, in the book at that stage would be walking free and whistling to herself because she was, as it were, unencumbered and free and able to walk. So it was that sense. A sort of image of a woman walking off into the future, able to whistle. But beyond that there was the sense that I wanted to inhabit a world where women did things that men did, and men did things that women did, and there wasn't a strict differentiation of what women could and couldn't do. There were an enormous number of things, even when I started this book, that women couldn't do: they weren't allowed into the Union at Cambridge University; there were a lot of jobs they weren't allowed to have. There is almost nothing now. There has been a lot of political achievement, although *A Whistling Woman* ends before most of that happened.

But I don't think I ever had any doubt that it would happen. Even in the 1950s it seemed to me that women were going to take a step here, take a step there, seize a little bit of ground. I didn't feel violently oppressed. I just felt that I was part of a process that was moving forward. And in fact I felt, in many ways, more oppressed by the expectations of the women's movement.

JN: You used an interesting expression there when you said that you wanted to 'inhabit' a world. It's an idea that comes into the end of *A Whistling Woman* – the idea of literature as a kind of parallel world – 'She thought about her life. She found herself thinking about *Paradise Lost*' [p. 420]. It's an idea that comes back again and again, doesn't it?

ASB: I think Milton did think of it that way. This is almost a private thing, but I will say it for this interview even so, because it is about reading. I think Milton saw Paradise as art, because he was blind, partly. He had this brightly coloured world in his head, that was intensely more alive than the world he was in, that was full of revolution and restriction and daughters whom he bashed about and made read aloud to him. And I've always thought that a lot of the English literature I care about comes in a direct line out of *Paradise Lost*. You go from *Paradise Lost* through to [Wordsworth's] *The Prelude*, and even through to [the poet] Wallace Stevens in America, and there's a sense of the lost paradise garden, and [Samuel Taylor Coleridge's poem] 'Kubla Khan' is a version of it. There's a lost paradise garden, where you might wander. 'There is a little garden close / Set thick with lily and red rose / Where I would wander if I might, / From dewy dawn to dewy night, / And have one with me wandering . . .' That's [William] Morris – and the 'dewy dawn' is actually out of *Paradise Lost* – most of it is. And so *Paradise Lost* itself, with its closed wall around a perfect garden, which I see as a kind of intensely beautiful medieval illumination, is my image of all the seeing and thinking and beautiful things that there were in the past, as opposed to the vein of language running through your blood which is still going on.

And I was quite distressed when I got to the end of *A*

Whistling Woman to realise how much it now mattered to me that the science of *Paradise Lost* was so hopelessly wrong. You know – it does invalidate it a little bit. But I like the ending of *A Whistling Woman* because I did manage to get the end of *Paradise Lost* in there unobtrusively, if people don't recognise it – and totally obtrusively, if they do!

JN: The novel begins with the storytelling by Agatha – it's a sort of fairy story about trolls – which she finishes, and annoys her audience because she finishes the story that's been running for so long, and I did wonder if you were going to do something similar – whether you were going to continually deny your readers an ending? But you say you have, in fact, now finished the quartet?

ASB: I have finished it. And I put that ending as a beginning as a kind of challenge to myself, to make myself finish it, and to make it be a finished object. I thought, if it announces at the beginning that this is a book about endings, everybody will read it under the shadow of this rather sudden ending, and with any luck they won't ask me to write any more. The first one in the quartet [*The Virgin in the Garden*] takes place in 1953, but actually opens with a prologue in 1968. And the second one [*Still Life*] has a prologue set at the [1980] post-Impressionist exhibition which actually takes place after the end of the fourth one [*A Whistling Woman*]. So the novels sort of cast shadows forwards – the whole four novels – saying this life went on beyond the end of this artificial volume book, or book in four volumes.

But, nevertheless, the end of the fourth novel is the end of a story, and George Eliot once said, 'The endings of novels are always the most unsatisfactory things about them', and the ending of a quartet is a very difficult thing to orchestrate – particularly if you aren't musical!

JN: But it does finish with this idea of a new space, a new world, and new risks. So yes, the quartet is over, but the characters – one is led to believe – will continue.

ASB: Yes, I had always wanted *not* to write a certain kind of ending. All the novels I read in the 1950s ended up with somebody having had some dreadful experience and, having cast it off, were now a sort of cleanly washed new being, standing on the threshold of a door peering out to a new world. The archetype is [D. H. Lawrence's] *Sons and Lovers*, but also Rosamond Lehmann's *Dusty Answer*, where the whole of the story is finished and the person is still young and about to start possibly living.

And I terribly wanted not to write an ending like that. I like books that *end*. But I think this one does end because it ends with a lot of romantic coming together, which may or may not be permanent, but are certainly ends of those particular bits of plots for those characters.

That was something that I learned from Iris Murdoch. That the artificial ending of a Shakespeare comedy is a very, very beautiful object. It isn't just unreal. It's unreal for very good reasons. Human beings have always told themselves stories with temporary artificial endings where people are all right. I wanted my quartet to have most of my people, who were not dead, all right. I wanted them to be poised for a moment in the kind of happiness you can leave people in in a story. Because it's just as sentimental to make them all unhappy and dissatisfied. It's just as untrue to stop at that sort of moment.

Death is a proper ending, but if you don't kill your characters then you have a right to a happy ending.

VINTAGE
LIVING
TEXTS

Possession

IN CLOSE-UP

Reading guides for

POSSESSION

BEFORE YOU BEGIN TO READ . . .
— Read the interview with Byatt. You will see there that she identifies a number of themes and techniques:

- Possession
- Poetry
- Metaphor
- Names and naming
- Colour

Other themes that may be useful to consider while reading the novel include:

- Ownership
- The archive
- Past and present
- Knowing and unknowing
- Cryptic clues

Reading activities: detailed analysis

Focus on: the title

CONSIDER THE CONNOTATIONS . . .

— Before you begin to read, think about the title of *Possession*. What does this interesting word suggest to you and what expectations does it set up? Is it an abstract noun (as in 'ownership' or 'control'), or a concrete one (as in 'a possession'), or possibly both? The words 'possession' and 'ownership' have rather different connotations. You might compare them. How is the noun 'a possession' linked to notions of wealth and control?

— Now think of the language we use to describe possession: 'an act of possession', 'to take possession', 'to claim possession'. Consider what it means when a person is described as 'possessed', or 'self-possessed'.

— Be aware of how the title takes on new meanings as you read the novel, and whenever you come across words or ideas suggesting possession during your reading of the novel, make a note of them. This is one way to build up a picture of the theme of possession in the novel. You might like to consider as you read whether it is apt that the title of this novel could be both abstract and concrete.

COMPARE AND CONSIDER . . .
— Think of other novels that use one-word titles, especially of those that use abstract nouns. Examples might include Ian McEwan's *Atonement*, J. M. Coetzee's *Disgrace* or Pat Barker's *Regeneration*. What is the effect on the expectations of the reader of such titles? Does the broad suggestiveness of such titles draw a reader in? McEwan originally intended to call his novel *An Atonement*, but changed the title at proof stage. Consider how the absence of the indefinite article creates different effects in both *Atonement* and *Possession*.

Focus on: the dedication

RESEARCH AND CONSIDER . . .
— *Possession* is dedicated to Isobel Armstrong, an eminent writer and critic, and a professor of English literature who specialises in the study of Victorian poetry. One of her many books is entitled *Language as Living Form in Nineteenth-century Poetry* (1982). There are moments in *Possession* where the processes and effects of literary language are discussed, by the two poets in the nineteenth-century story, and by the two academics in the twentieth-century story. How important to *Possession* is the idea of language as a 'living' form? If you can, read *Language as Living Form* to gain a clearer sense of what this expression might mean. Make a note of the points where reference is made to that concept, and note down any places where you think that the language of this novel – including the poetic parts of it – can be said to be 'living'.

Focus on: the epigraphs

ANALYSE AND MAKE CONNECTIONS . . .

— Look carefully at the two epigraphs, the first from the preface to a novel by the American writer Nathaniel Hawthorne (1804–1864), and the second from a work by the English poet Robert Browning (1812–1889). What can you see immediately in the extracts themselves that may make them appropriate choices for preceding this novel? As you read, return to them occasionally and consider their significance again. If you have the time, read either, or both, Hawthorne's novel and Browning's poem and make connections between those works and Byatt's novel.

CHAPTER ONE
(pp. 1–8)

Focus on: openings

COMPARE AND ASSESS . . .

— In a certain way this novel has two openings: the poetry quoting a work written by the fictional author Randolph Henry Ash, and the beginning of the prose story. What is appropriate about each of these? The first refers to a garden – which garden? Might there be more than one garden? The second beginning refers to a book. Why is this appropriate? Treat these first pages of the novel as if they are one of those picture puzzles where you have to spot hidden images. How many books can you find in this passage? Include books explicitly mentioned, or only implied or alluded to. Which of these would appear on your list?

● A volume of Randolph Henry Ash's poetry
● A cookbook
● The Bible

- Stories from classical mythology
- A volume on car maintenance
- *Hello!* magazine
- A book of pornography

Focus on: imagery of the living and the dead

LIST AND ANALYSE . . .

— Look over these pages and note down all the words that are associated with death and with bringing things back to life. When you have your list, consider how the image of resurrection or reanimation is used in these pages. When you have begun to read on, ask yourself why this is an appropriate image for the beginning of this particular story. By the time you have reached the end of the novel, you will be aware that there are many ways in which this image is woven through it.

Focus on: colour

KEEP A NOTE . . .

— Make a list of the colours that appear in this section. You will need it later on.

Focus on: letters

COMPARE AND CONTRAST . . .

— Analyse the two drafts of Ash's letter that Roland finds. What are the differences between them? Jot down your impressions of the writer's state of mind.

— If you don't object to reading ahead a little (and you might prefer to let the story unfold in its own way), turn to p. 86 where you will find the version of the letter that Ash actually sent. Compare that version with the two drafts. How much of the writer's feelings – as evidenced in the drafts – is left in the sent version?

— Finally, if you turn to the Contexts section for *Possession*, (on p. 98) you will find an extract from the first letter that the real poet Robert Browning wrote to his fellow poet Elizabeth Barrett in 1845. They were married in September 1846. How does this real letter compare with these fictional letters? Look up the term 'allusion' in the glossary of literary terms and consider the effects created by the use of allusion. Is Byatt using allusion here, and if so, to what effect?

Focus on: Victorian literary history

REFER AND REFLECT . . .
— How many real people are named in these opening pages? Begin by noting the ones you have heard of and jot down whatever you happen to know about them. If you are not sure, look up the name in a biographical dictionary or a companion to English literature and sort out the historical characters from the fictional ones. Then consider whether you really need this information. Is there enough told to you in the book itself? Or does the added recognition enrich your reading? If so, in what ways?

CHAPTER TWO
(pp. 9–21)

Focus on: names and naming

PLAY WITH IDEAS . . .
— If you look at the interview with Byatt, (on pp. 16–17) you will see that she speaks about names and, in particular, discusses the fact that she planned out the allusions in Christabel's surname of 'LaMotte' and Maud's surname of 'Bailey'. Consider other names in the novel. What ideas are suggested by Ash, Randolph, Christabel, Maud, Blackadder, Cropper,

Roland, Wolff or Stern? Which names have a historical or literary significance? Which names have an allusive or metaphorical implication?

Focus on: grammar and grammatical constructions

PARSE . . .
— Chapter Two is introduced with a quotation from Randolph Henry Ash (p. 9). Parse this paragraph: that is, work through it, jotting down which word is which part of speech. So it begins 'A man' (= subject) 'is' (= verb) 'the history of' (=adjectival phrase), and so on. If you are unsure about grammatical terms and definitions, refer to *Grammar and Writing*, Rebecca Stott and Peter Chapman, eds (2001).
— What do you notice about the grammatical style of this quotation? Consider how many subordinate phrases there are. Consider how many qualifications and lists are used. What are the effects of these aspects of style?

COMPARE AND CONSIDER . . .
— Read these two famous passages from Walter Pater's 'Conclusion' to *Studies in the History of the Renaissance* (1873).

A counted number of pulses is given to us only of a variegated, dramatic life. How may we see in them all that is to be seen in them by the finest senses? How can we pass most swiftly from point to point, and be present always at the focus where the greatest number of vital forces unite in their purest energy? To burn always with this hard, gemlike flame, to maintain this ecstasy, is success in life.

Not to discriminate every moment some passionate attitude in those about us, and in the brilliance of their gifts some tragic dividing of forces on their

ways is, on this short day of frost and sun, to sleep
before evening.

— First, compare the grammar and syntax of Pater's prose with
that of the fictional Ash. Second, compare the themes and the
argument in the two passages. Then ask yourself how Roland's
description and assessment of Ash's prose (p. 9) matches up to
your own perception of its method. Finally, look at p. 20 where
the narrative comes back to the question of Ash's syntax and,
again, ask yourself how Roland's image of 'stalking' Ash through
his grammatical style matches up to your experience of reading
Ash – in poetry (p. 1) and in prose (p. 9). Keep the idea of
'stalking' Ash in your mind as you continue to read.

Focus on: multiple identities

NOTE AND ASSESS . . .
— On p. 14 the novel reads, 'There were now two Vals.' On
p. 15 we are told that 'Roland possessed three images of
Randolph Henry Ash'. Consider each of these examples of multiple incarnations. How far is it possible for people to 'possess'
more than one identity? When you have read on, ask yourself
how far this is a theme for the novel overall.

Focus on: cabinets of curiosities

INVESTIGATE . . .
— Look at p. 16 where the many items in the background of
Ash's portrait are described. Consider this eclectic list of objects.
Then find out about cabinets of curiosities. You might like to
read *Cabinets of Curiosities* (2002) by Patrick Mauriès which
illustrates the most exotic items these rooms of wonders contained. Many items were genuinely scientific, such as stuffed
or preserved animals and plants, or minerals and fossils. Some
were merely curious, some grotesque, such as freaks of nature

and monstrous births. Man-made items were mixed in, such as wax effigies, death masks, or intricate mechanical automata that imitated living things. You might like to go and look at one of these rooms, such as that in the Brighton Museum or in the Tate Modern. Once you have some idea of what they are, and when and why they were important, keep that notion in mind and watch out for more of them in *Possession*. Eventually, you should ask yourself how the larger idea of the 'cabinet of curiosities' might relate to the themes of the novel as a whole.

Focus on: gardens

LOOK FOR A PATTERN . . .
— Mrs Irving's garden is forbidden to Roland and Val (pp. 17–18). How does this relate to other gardens that you have already encountered in the novel?

CHAPTER THREE
(pp. 22–34)

Focus on: analogies

RELATE . . .
— Look at the first paragraph of this chapter. How does it relate to the theme of cabinets of curiosities? Where else in this chapter does the analogy occur?

Focus on: imagery

IDENTIFY . . .
— When you have read the chapter, ask yourself what the relevance of the 'quotation' from Ash is to the setting and the people we encounter in this chapter. Think about names as well as images and circumstances.

Focus on: God, Men and Heroes *or* Men and Women

RESEARCH AND COMPARE . . .

— Crabb Robinson's description of Randolph Ash's fictional collection of poems entitled *God, Men and Heroes* (pp. 23–4) suggests an allusion to Robert Browning's (real) collection of poems called *Men and Women* (1855). Browning was a poet who specialised in the 'dramatic monologue', a form in which one character speaks in an extended soliloquy or conversation – and gives away more than he means to about himself. Browning's famous dramatic monologues include 'My Last Duchess', 'Childe Roland to the Dark Tower Came' and 'Porphyria's Lover'. Look at any one of these poems, or look at the collection *Men and Women*, and compare Browning's method with that of Ash as described by Crabb Robinson.

Focus on: history and fiction

RESEARCH . . .

— Again, on pp. 24–5, several real historical figures are mentioned among the fictional characters. Walter Bagehot and Anna Jameson, for instance, were real. Discriminate between those you know to be real from those who are not. How much do you know about these historical figures? If you don't know them, find out about them using a biographical dictionary or the Internet.

Focus on: the theme of authenticity

TRANSCRIBE . . .

— Take any of the literary passages in the book – the poetry quotation on p. 1, for instance – and transcribe it. Then get somebody else to check the accuracy of your transcription. Did you get it 100 per cent right, or not? How accurate were you?

Cropper makes his students do this exercise and 'There was never an error-free text' (p. 25). How might this question of accuracy – or, rather, lack of it – relate to the theme of authenticity and scholarship that runs through the whole of the book?

Focus on: libraries

VISIT . . .
— On p. 26 Roland walks through the old Reading Room in the British Museum. This is the third library we have seen so far in the novel. The British Museum was, until 1997, the home of the British Library, which is an official copyright library as well as the holder of many precious manuscripts. The British Library is now in its own specially created building at St Pancras in London. Even so, the collection is so huge that many books are still housed in depositories. You can visit the old Reading Room, which was the place where many eminent people have studied, including Karl Marx. In the British Museum shop one can buy *The British Museum Reading Room* by Marjorie Caygill, which gives an insight into the room's history.

OR ELSE COMPARE . . .
— Read the sections in Virginia Woolf's *A Room of One's Own* (1929) where she describes the Reading Room. What are the differences between Woolf's and Roland's (or Byatt's) descriptions?

Focus on: the theme of ventriloquism

INTERPRET AND RELATE . . .
— On p. 27, Roland describes Ash's poetic technique as one of 'ventriloquism'. This word can designate not only voice projection, but all the various forms taken by sourceless, displaced and dissociated voices. What does it mean to speak 'for' or 'through' somebody else? If you look at the interview

(on pp. 18–20, 28) you will see that Byatt talks about the role of the novelist being like a kind of ventriloquism. This term suggests a mobility of voice, but also calls into question that voice's authoritative origin (note that the word 'authority' has the same roots as the word 'author'). How does this theme relate to the novel as a whole so far? (Refer to the Contexts section (on p. 100) for a further exercise on ventriloquism.)

Focus on: the key to all mythologies

RESEARCH AND COMPARE . . .
— In George Eliot's *Middlemarch* (1871–2), Casaubon has made it his life's work to compile a 'key to all mythologies'. Read the opening of Chapter 10 of *Middlemarch* and compare Blackadder's account of LaMotte's work (p. 31) with that of Casaubon.

Focus on: fairy tales

NOTE THE CHARACTERISATION . . .
— Wolff by name, and wolf by nature. Look at the description of Fergus Wolff on p. 32, and note the comparison. What other wolf appears in this section? (Refer to the Contexts section (on p. 101) for a further exercise on wolves in fairy tales.)

RESEARCH . . .
— Wolff gives Roland a short account of Christabel LaMotte's *The Fairy Melusina* (p. 33). What fairy tales do you recognise here? Once you have made your own list, look up:

● Lamia
● Ondine
● Medusa

What use has Byatt made of any or all of these stories?

CHAPTER FOUR
(pp. 35–67)

Focus on: poetry

READ AND COMPARE . . .
— Refer to any of these three poems by Christina Rossetti (1830–1894): 'In an Artist's Studio', 'Winter: My Secret', 'A Birthday'. Read the poem by the fictional Christabel LaMotte on p. 35 and then compare its diction, tone, vocabulary and poetic form with one or all of the Rossetti poems. How does this help you to place Christabel's style of poetry?

Focus on: colour

KEEP A NOTE . . .
— Jot down all the descriptions involving colour in this chapter. You will need them later. Byatt speaks about her use of colour, in this and others of her novels, in the interview (on pp. 14–16).

Focus on: Christabel

COMPARE AND CONNECT LITERARY ALLUSIONS . . .
— On p. 45, we learn through Blanche Glover's journal that she is painting a picture called 'Christabel before Sir Leoline'. The reference is to Christabel's name, and her name is a reference to a poem called 'Christabel' by Samuel Taylor Coleridge. Read that poem and make a note of as many themes as you can that might connect that poem with this novel.
— Look at the account of the posters in the Senior Common Room coffee room (p. 48). What relates these words to Christabel's story and to the themes and allusions in the novel so far? Make a note to come back to this question when you have read to the end of the novel.

Focus on: the sibyl

RESEARCH . . .
— Find out about the sibyls, who they were, and where they appear in Greek mythology and in literature. The sibyl most frequently referred to in the Greek tradition is that of Cumae who, like Pythia of Delphi, was an oracle of Apollo. These inspired women prophets later became synonymous with darkly oracular pronouncements. How might these mythical figures relate to the themes of *Possession*?

Focus on: literary theory and feminist criticism

RESEARCH AND COMPARE . . .
— Maud describes one of her own papers on the poetry of Christabel LaMotte. If you are interested in the ways that the novel reinterprets, reinvents and plays with contemporary feminist criticism, look up the collection of essays called *Victorian Women Poets: A Critical Reader*, edited by Angela Leighton (1996). For a brief definition of the terms employed in feminist theory and criticism, refer to a dictionary of literary theory.

COMPARE AND CONNECT . . .
— Read Christabel's story of 'The Glass Coffin' on pp. 58–67. Focus particularly on:

● The image of the coffin
● The lady's insistence on 'giving herself of her own free will'
● Her enforced silence

— How might this inset story, and these elements in particular, relate a) to the stories of Christabel and Maud, b) to the themes of the novel as a whole, and c) to the terms of feminist criticism?

49

CHAPTER FIVE
(pp. 68–91)

Focus on: the immured lady

COMPARE AND CONTRAST . . .
— Read Alfred, Lord Tennyson's poems 'The Lady of Shalott' and 'Mariana'. How do the images of isolation and enchantment in those poems illuminate your reading of this section about Christabel's family home?

Focus on: memorials

EXAMINE . . .
— Look at the text of the memorial engraved on Christabel's tombstone (p. 70). Then think about Maud's assessment of this text (p. 71). Find out about the text engraved on Jane Austen's tomb in Winchester Cathedral. Apply Maud's principles to Austen's epitaphs. In what ways does her assessment apply to both inscriptions?

Focus on: characterisation

INTERPRET . . .
— Roland rescues Lady Bailey when her wheelchair becomes stuck (pp. 72–3). How does this episode affect your idea of Roland's character so far? How does his 'rescue' of a trapped lady relate to the themes of the novel as a whole?

Focus on: allusion and reference

FIND OUT . . .
— If you do not already know it, find out about the 'laundry list' (p. 82) in Jane Austen's novel *Northanger Abbey* (1818).

COUNT UP . . .
— How many references to fairy tales – their terms and their tellers – can you find in this chapter? Why might they be relevant?

LOOK BACK AND RESEARCH . . .
— On p. 85 a print in Christabel's room is mentioned and it is a copy of Lord Leighton's Proserpina. Look back at p. 1 where Proserpina also figures. Who was she? If you don't know, look her up in a dictionary of classical mythology. She is sometimes given the name of Persephone. Why is her story important to the themes of *Possession* – and to the overall idea of 'possession'? Remember that you considered the themes of death and resurrection in relation to the first chapter.

— Then look ahead to p. 125 where you will see that Persephone is mentioned again. When you get to that part of the novel, consider the ways in which Val might be another 'Proserpina' figure.

CHAPTER SIX
(pp. 92–111)

Focus on: irony

CONSIDER AND ASSESS . . .
— In this chapter we meet Mortimer Cropper and on p. 93 we are told, 'This was not his milieu.' Read over pp. 92–7, paying particular attention to the exchanges between Cropper and Daisy Wapshott. What means are used to signal the tension between their two worlds? How is irony used to point up the contrast? What is your own attitude to Cropper as a result?

Focus on: clichés

TRANSFORM . . .

'He calculated that the richest dreams of her modest avarice would be unlikely to reach the sort of sum he would willingly pay on the open market' (p. 97). 'I am rich beyond the dreams of avarice' is a quotation from *The Gamester*, a play by Edward Moore (1712–1757). But it has also become a cliché and a 'dead metaphor' which – in this particular case – Byatt brings back to life by describing Daisy's 'modest avarice'.

— Write an account of the plot of *Possession* so far using as many clichés as you can. Use an online dictionary of clichés for ideas. Your account might begin: 'Once upon a time Henry Randolph Ash was flavour of the month . . .' When you have finished, write your plot out again, but this time, replace every cliché with a considered and appropriate phrase.

Focus on: the cabinet of curiosities

ASK YOURSELF . . .

— How does Mortimer Cropper's parents' Treasure Cabinet connect to the theme of the cabinet of curiosities in the novel as a whole?

Focus on: history and fiction

RESEARCH . . .

— Use the Internet to find out about these real historical figures:

- Robert Owen
- Jefferson
- Swedenborg
- Honoré de Balzac
- Julia Margaret Cameron
- Elizabeth Gaskell

— What light (if any) does your research throw on Byatt's use of allusions?

RESEARCH AND RELATE . . .
— On pp. 101–2 mention is made of the principles of Robert Owen and Charles Fourier, and of the attempt to set up a phalanstery in New Mexico. These early experiments and theories about communal living are based on real events and publications. Read Barbara Taylor's *Eve and the New Jerusalem* (1983) for an account of Owen's work. You will find extracts from Charles Fourier's writings in Elizabeth Barrett Browning's *Aurora Leigh*, edited by Margaret Reynolds (1996). Consider how these examples of ideas concerning communal living and new ways of developing social relations might be connected to the themes of the novel as a whole.

COMPARE . . .
— Read this extract from one of Elizabeth Barrett Browning's letters to her sister. It tells of an occasion during the journey that the Brownings made, soon after their marriage in 1846, through France, journeying by boat down the Rhône and on to Italy.

> The wild, striking scenery . . . the fantastic rocks &
> ruined castles we could only see by painful glimpses
> through the loophole windows of the miserable cabin
> – wasn't it unfortunate? At Avignon . . . We stayed
> there three or four days, & made a pilgrimage to
> Vaucluse as became poets, & my spirits rose & the
> enjoyment of the hour spent at the sacred fountain
> was complete. It stands deep & still & green against
> a majestic wall of rock, & then falls, boils, breaks,
> foams over the stones, down into the channel of the
> little river winding away greenly, greenly – the great

green desolate precipices guarding it out of sight – A few little cypresses, & olive trees – no other tree in sight – All desolate & grand. R. said 'Ba, are you losing your senses?' – because without a word I made my way over the boiling water to a still rock in the middle of it . . . but he followed me & helped me, & we both sate in the spray, till Mrs. Jameson was provoked to make a sketch of us . . .
16–19 October, 1846.

— Now read Mortimer Cropper's account of the Ashes' wedding journey on pp. 108–9. What transformations has Byatt made here? And why are Cropper's allusions to mermaids and water-goddesses appropriate to the themes of the novel as a whole?

Focus on: spiritualism

RESEARCH AND RELATE . . .
— Read Robert Browning's poem 'Mr Sludge, "the Medium"'. Robert Browning famously did not much approve of the mid-nineteenth-century craze for spiritualism, while his wife, Elizabeth Barrett, was very intrigued. On one occasion they both witnessed a seance held by a well-known medium called Daniel Dunglass Hume, and it is sometimes thought that he was the original for 'Mr Sludge'. How does the theme of seances and spiritualism relate to the themes of the book so far? This will be returned to. Note that Byatt speaks about this theme in the interview (p. 28).

CHAPTER SEVEN
(pp. 112–27)

Focus on: naming

UNDERLINE AND ASK YOURSELF . . .

— Think about Beatrice Nest. Concentrate first of all on her surname and underline or jot down each word or phrase that might match up with this name and the concept of nesting. Is there anything here that might connect her with what you know of the images surrounding Christabel? Then consider the name 'Beatrice', which is the Italian form of Beatrix. This name derives from *Viatrix*, the feminine form of a Latin name meaning 'voyager' or 'traveller' (the spelling was altered by the association with the Latin for 'blessed' – *beatus*). Beatrice was Dante's guide in *The Divine Comedy* (1308–1321), and Benedick's sparring partner in Shakespeare's *Much Ado About Nothing* (c. 1599). What do her names suggest about her function in the novel?

Focus on: the image of the voyeur

CONSIDER . . .

— In Ellen Ash's account of her reading of *The Fairy Melusina* she mentions the moment when 'the husband, a man of insufficient faith, bores his peephole and observes his *Siren-spouse* at play in her vat of waters' (p. 121). Keep this image in mind – you will need it later. In the meantime, consider what terms the idea of the voyeur invokes. Who are the voyeurs in this novel? Are you, as a reader, also a voyeur?

CHAPTER EIGHT
(pp. 128–49)

Focus on: colour

KEEP A NOTE . . .

— Pay attention to the imagery of colour throughout this chapter. Match it up with your previous notes and begin to work out what overall use is being made of colour. Are any particular colours associated with any particular characters?

Focus on: unheimlich

READ AND APPLY . . .

— Read Sigmund Freud's essay 'The Uncanny' (1919), a psychoanalytic reading of E. T. A. Hoffman's supernatural tale 'The Sandman'. Consider his definition of 'homely' and 'unhomely'. In English the equivalent word for the German *unheimlich* is 'uncanny'. Look up the word 'uncanny' in the *Oxford English Dictionary*. When you have all these pieces of information, relate them to the letter which Randolph Ash writes to Christabel (pp. 131–3).

Focus on: the image of glass

EXPLORE THE ASSOCIATIONS . . .

— There are several references to glass and the various properties of glass in this chapter, and especially from p. 133 on. Work through this list of the attributes of glass. Which seems to you the most significant or important?

- Transparency
- Delicacy
- Fragility
- Preciousness

- Light-giving
- Dangerous when broken
- Shard-like
- Blocking

— Now write a list of any attributes that you think may be missing. Then look over the whole chapter and consider where, when and why the image of glass and its various attributes may appear.

Focus on: the image of the voyeur

LOOK BACK, ASSESS AND COMPARE . . .
— On p. 147 Roland tries – for perfectly decent reasons – to see into the bathroom he shares with Maud. Look back at the end of the last chapter where the question of the voyeur was raised, first of all in relation to Ellen Ash's reading of Christabel's *The Fairy Melusina* and then in relation to you, the reader of this novel.
— How does this passage add to your perceptions of both these cases?

CHAPTER NINE
(pp. 150–6)

Focus on: the threshold

LINK . . .
— Where in the novel have we met the idea of the threshold before now? Remember that 'liminal' means 'on the border' or 'on the threshold'.

Focus on: fairy tales and the three caskets

READ AND COMPARE . . .

— Read Act 3 scene 2 of Shakespeare's *The Merchant of Venice* where Bassanio is asked to choose one of three caskets made of gold, silver and lead. How does that scene illuminate your reading of this story?

Focus on: the number 3

CONSIDER STRUCTURE . . .

— What is the cultural significance of the number 3? Consider the following statements:

- God's attributes are omniscience, omnipresence and omnipotence.
- The Holy Trinity is the Father, the Son and the Holy Spirit.
- Time is divided into past, present and future.
- English grammar expresses all relationships through three persons.
- Human capability comprises thought, word and deed.
- The simplest argument requires three propositions: the major premise, the minor premise and the conclusion. Hegalian dialectic comprises thesis, antithesis, synthesis.

— Three is a number with associations of completeness and perfection. Investigate the symbolism of the number 3 using a dictionary of symbolism. Consider the relevance of these ideas to this chapter.

CHAPTER TEN
(pp. 157–201)

Focus on: narrative structure

ASK YOURSELF . . .

— In this chapter we get to read the correspondence between Randolph Henry Ash and Christabel LaMotte. This series of letters is situated at a point approaching the centre of the book. Why might that be appropriate for the balance and structure of the novel as a whole?

Focus on: images

LIST . . .

— How many different images – already encountered in the novel – are built up here? Spiders are one. How many more can you find?

Focus on: letters

RESEARCH AND ANALYSE . . .

— In twenty months between 1845 and 1846 Robert Browning and Elizabeth Barrett exchanged 574 love letters. Read some (or all) of these letters and consider how that correspondence has been rewritten and reinvented by this (fictional) correspondence.

Focus on: intimacy

DISCERN . . .

— In reading these letters of lovers long since dead, how can you decipher the growing intimacy between them? Can you guess at what has happened by the end of the correspondence (p. 201)?

CHAPTER ELEVEN
(pp. 202–9)

Focus on: pastiche and pattern

COMPARE AND INTERPRET . . .

— Most of Chapter Ten was taken up with the correspondence between Randolph and Christabel. This whole chapter is taken up by Ash's poem. Why? What does the juxtaposition suggest to you about poetry and experience?

CHAPTER TWELVE
(pp. 210–38)

Focus on: the idea of the house

ASK YOURSELF . . .

— This chapter begins with a quotation from Christabel, 'What is a House?' (p. 210). Begin by asking yourself the same question. What does the idea of a house mean to you? Is it a place of safety, or a place of incarceration? What is the difference between a house and a home? If you did the exercise on '*unheimlich*' for Chapter Eight, look back at that and add your ideas there to the mix. Then look over this chapter and count how many houses – and homes – appear, and assess the different ideas and images they represent.

Focus on: verbal echoes

CONNECT . . .

— On p. 216, Blanche describes herself as a 'superfluous person'. On p. 218, Val uses the same words of herself. Later on in this chapter a third woman speaks about 'excluded persons'. Find that reference. Why might it be relevant that these three women are brought together thematically with this verbal echo?

PUT TOGETHER AGAIN . . .
— On p. 237, Maud – who knows Christabel's poetry well – recognises a phrase quoted by Roland – who knows Randolph's poetry well. The shared phrase in Randolph and Christabel's poetry suggests either a deliberate quotation, or some shared idea or experience. How might this literary parallel connect to the verbal parallel that the narrative has already set up between three, otherwise unconnected, characters?

CHAPTER THIRTEEN
(pp. 239–61)

Focus on: literary criticism

CRITICALLY EVALUATE . . .
— Take the two – very different – examples of a pastiche of literary criticism in this chapter. The first is supposed to be taken from Leonora Stern's work on LaMotte (pp. 243–6), and the second is supposed to be taken from Mortimer Cropper's biography of Ash (pp. 246–50). Treat each as if it were a piece of real literary criticism that you have been asked to assess. Jot down an outline of the argument, or the method of presentation, and then assess the persuasiveness of each. Note that you can resort to Roland's and Maud's assessments, set out in the text, to measure your own. But do that afterwards.

Focus on: naming

RELATE . . .
— On p. 252, Roland and Maud discuss the significance of

naming and playing with names in the work of their two poets. Look back over your notes on naming and relate this passage to the theme in the novel as a whole.

READ FURTHER . . .

— Ash is a poet who is supposed to play with and pun on his own name. John Donne (1572–1631) did the same, punning both on his own name, and on the name of his wife Ann More. Read Donne's poem 'A Hymne to God the Father' or his poem 'Sappho to Philaenis', and consider the ways in which Donne may be punning on these two names.

Focus on: metaphors

LOOK UP AND ASSESS . . .

— On p. 253, Roland and Maud discuss how metaphors work. In the interview (p. 25) Byatt speaks about metaphor and why it is so compelling. Make sure you understand what a metaphor is. Look it up in the glossary or in a dictionary of literary terms. Then consider how the image of the metaphor may relate to the themes and the structure of the novel as a whole. Why might it be significant that the novel has many layers? These might include: the nineteenth-century story, the twentieth-century story, the pastiches of a variety of literary forms and the voice of the omniscient narrator.

CONSIDER THE ALLUSION . . .

— The woman in the shop selling Whitby jet appreciates Maud's brooch (pp. 258–61). Maud had retrieved it from the dressing-up box because it reminded her of the Little Mermaid, then, later, of Christabel's poem *The Fairy Melusina*. If you don't know the story of the Little Mermaid, then look it up. It was written by Hans Christian Andersen. Consider how the story may illuminate what you know of Christabel's story so far.

CHAPTER FOURTEEN
(pp. 262–72)

Focus on: the image of water

NOTE AND COMMENT . . .
— There are several pictures and images of water, waterfalls and pools in this chapter. Make a note of as many as you can find and the kinds of things they might signify. Then ask yourself where and how the image of water has been used elsewhere in the novel.

Focus on: colour

LINK . . .
— Which colours are important in this chapter? How do they connect to other such colour-coding in the novel as a whole?

CHAPTER FIFTEEN
(pp. 273–88)

Focus on: the epigraph

ASSESS . . .
— As ever, the epigraph to this chapter is a quotation from one of Randolph Henry Ash's imaginary poems – invented and composed by Byatt. Consider what this extract suggests to you just on its own merits. Why, for instance, are two words in italics? Then – when you have read the chapter through – consider how the poetic extract relates to the events therein. Remember that Byatt has composed this poetic extract, before, or after, or during the time when she was writing the chapter

63

to which it is attached. Assess in what ways she has manipulated our reactions in this process.

Focus on: narrative structure and method

EXAMINE AND CONSIDER . . .

— Think carefully about the ways in which this chapter has been constructed. We have some idea of who these people are. We also have some idea of what is going to happen. And yet the narrative method here carefully distances us. How does it achieve that? It may be simple things like the fact that we begin the chapter with a reference to 'The man and the woman' – as if we hadn't already met them before in the story. It may be the use of the third person and the omniscient narrator simply speaking of 'he' that makes the distance. Try to work out why these strategies affect you and how.

LOOK AT THE WORDING . . .

— Notice the way in which many short clauses and sentences are used in building towards a climax in this chapter. Look at p. 280, 'They walked by the sea', or p. 281, 'The time came nearer', or p. 285, 'They were good days.' How does this pared-down style help to create the climax of feeling?

DISCRIMINATE . . .

— Why do you suppose that the omniscient narrator filters the storytelling perspective through Ash in parts of this chapter? Work out which sections are – as it were – 'pure' omniscient narrator, and which tell us things that only Ash himself could know.

TRANSFORM . . .

— We never hear Christabel's direct voice in this chapter, except in fragments of dialogue. Nor do we have the omniscient narrator speaking from her point of view. Write one scene from this episode from Christabel's point of view: it could be written either in the first person, or in the third person but from her perspective. Consider how often or not you have heard Christabel's point of view so far.

NOTICE . . .
— This is a book that runs to 511 pages. We are just past halfway through here. Why might it be appropriate that this chapter is at the centre of the book?

Focus on: colour

COMPILE . . .
— On p. 277, Ash considers Christabel and her colours. Add this passage to any notes that you are keeping about the thematic function of colour in the novel as a whole. Note that on p. 274 we are told that Christabel is wearing green boots. Where might you have noticed this detail elsewhere?

Focus on: selkies

RESEARCH . . .
— On p. 280, Ash and LaMotte discuss the legend of the selkie or seal woman. An Internet search station will take you to the information you need to find out about this legend. How does it relate to the story being told here? And how does the imagery of water, of transformations, of strange animal wives married to humans connect to the themes of the novel as a whole?

EXAMINE AND ASSESS . . .
— If you look at the brief description of 'those long strange nights' on pp. 283–4, you will see that much of the imagery is based on water or sea pictures. Note down as many examples

as you can. Then consider how this imagery relates to a) the characterisation of Christabel in the novel as a whole, and b) the settings and the themes of the novel overall.

Focus on: the omniscient narrator

EXAMINE . . .

— In the interview (on pp. 20–21)Byatt speaks about the few occasions in the novel when the omniscient narrator intervenes to tell us things that only one character can know, and that would not otherwise be revealed. The ending is one such example, so you might consider that when you get there. Another happens here when we are told some of Randolph Henry Ash's private thoughts about Christabel and his sexual experience with and imagination of her (pp. 284–5). Think about why it is important to us as readers to know these things and to be made privy to his thoughts. What is the effect of this knowledge? How does it contribute to your understanding of and interest in Ash and Christabel?

Focus on: time and the meanings of time

READ MORE WIDELY AND COMPARE . . .

— 'He remembered most, when it was over, when time had run out, a day they had spent in a place called the Boggle Hole' (p. 286). 'Time' is a key word in this section. Later on, Randolph thinks of Christabel's form as if she were an 'hour-glass' (p. 287). On p. 284, he had woken to find Christabel weeping at the loss of 'time'. Think about time and the meanings that attach to time. Look up or try to remember other poems, or songs that use the word 'time'. Examples might include:

- 'They all have lied who told me time would heal' (Edna St Vincent Millay).

- 'I wasted time, and now doth time waste me' (Shakespeare's *Richard II*, Act 5, scene 5).

— Consider how the word 'time' means different things in each case here. Match these definitions to each of the above lines:

- 'The first occasion'
- 'The passage of time'
- 'Opportunities and possibilities'
- 'One day, whenever you have the chance'
- 'Make an arrangement to do something'

— Note that – while each of these examples employs different notions of what 'time' may be – each poem, speech and song mentioned here includes some kind of epiphany or special 'moment in time' and consciousness. Then look back at these passages in *Possession* and consider the ways in which the text uses the same or similar methods. Keep looking out for other places in the novel where time and its varied meanings are questioned and exploited.

CHAPTER SIXTEEN
(pp. 289–98)

Focus on: Victorian poetry

COMPARE . . .
— This section purports to be an extract from Christabel LaMotte's long narrative poem *The Fairy Melusine*. Byatt composed all the poems in *Possession* herself. She speaks about this in the interview (pp. 17–20). As an expert on Victorian literature, her pastiches draw upon her knowledge of writers such

as Tennyson, Robert Browning and Christina Rossetti. Read some (or all) of the following poems and look for points of comparison.

- Tennyson's 'The Lady of Shalott'
- Rossetti's 'Goblin Market'
- Robert Browning's 'Childe Roland to the Dark Tower Came'
- Elizabeth Barrett Browning's *Aurora Leigh*.

— None of these poems lies directly behind *The Fairy Melusine*, but you could pick out elements in the nineteenth-century works and in Byatt's reworking that include: the lady in the castle, hidden from the world (Tennyson); the strange and threatening landscape and the unknown quest (Browning); the fairy world (Rossetti); the contemplative poet considering her own role in writing (Barrett Browning).

RESEARCH THE CONTEXT . . .
— Many of the women poets working in the nineteenth century saw themselves, even at the time, as part of a particular tradition where they read each other's work and often wrote poems dedicated or referring to each other. Look at the collections *Nineteenth-Century Women Poets*, edited by Isobel Armstrong, Joseph Bristow and Cath Sharrock (1999), or *Victorian Women Poets*, edited by Angela Leighton and Margaret Reynolds (1998), to get an overview of this tradition.

Focus on: fairy tales and their tellers

EXTEND YOUR READING . . .
— A large number of poems and novels in the nineteenth century focused on fairy tales or stories for children. Well-known examples include Christina Rossetti's 'Goblin Market' and Charles Kingsley's *The Water Babies*. For the role of women as

the teller of fairy tales, read Marina Warner's *From the Beast to the Blonde: Fairy Tales and their Tellers* (1996).

Focus on: myth and metamorphosis

RESEARCH . . .

LaMotte's poem deals with change and metamorphosis. The term metamorphosis is from the Greek and means 'extraordinary transformation', 'meta' meaning above or beyond, and 'morphosis' meaning change. In Greek and Roman mythology it usually refers to cases where men and women are turned into beasts or other forms. The Roman poet Ovid, writing in the first century, composed a well-known series about such strange events called *Metamorphoses*.

— There are several mythological figures mentioned on p. 292 including: Psyche, Medusa, Scylla, Hecate, Hydra, the siren and the Sphinx. Even if you already know their stories, look them up in a dictionary of classical mythology – a good online dictionary will give you the information you need – as you may find unexpected elements in the stories. Then consider how any or all of these stories may relate to the events in *Possession*. Remember that both Randolph and Christabel have been 'changed' by their experience. Maud and Roland are soon also to be 'changed' by theirs.

Focus on: connections

IMAGINATIVELY RELATE . . .

— Look at the passages on pp. 296–8 that describe the lady in the poem who sits on a rock and sings to herself. Consider the ways in which this may be an image of Christabel herself. Look at the colours that are used to describe her (refer back to pp. 276–7). Look closely at the description of her face (and here you might like to refer back to Randolph's thoughts about Christabel's face on pp. 277–8). Then ask yourself how the events told here in the extract from the poem may connect to the events that we have just seen in the previous chapter – both literally (the Boggle Hole) and metaphorically (the quest, the arrival, the mutual discovery). It would also be a good idea to look back to Chapter Fourteen to see if you can make the same connections between the images and terms of the poem and Roland and Maud's experiences in Yorkshire.

DRAW UP LISTS . . .

— Here is a list of themes that relate both to the extract from the poem in this chapter, and to the novel as a whole. Take three of them and write down as many concrete circumstances or examples from the novel as you can that go with and support the playing out of these themes.

• Possession
• The quest
• Water
• Whiteness
• Secrets
• Transformation
• Objects and collections
• Knowledge
• Heritage and inheritance

CHAPTER SEVENTEEN
(pp. 299–305)

Focus on: spiritualism

RESEARCH . . .

During the 1840s and 1850s, many people were interested in the phenomena of spiritualism and there were several well-known mediums who travelled across Europe and America performing seances in private homes for those who were believers or simply curious. One such was the Scot Daniel Dunglass Home who in the 1860s, among other engagements, gave a seance which was attended by the poets Robert Browning and Elizabeth Barrett Browning who happened to be visiting England from their home in Italy. Elizabeth was much interested in the phenomenon; Robert was more sceptical. It is thought that his poem 'Mr Sludge, "the Medium"' may have been one result of this experience.

— Read that poem, or read some of Elizabeth Barrett's letter on the subject in ed. Scott Lewis, *The Letters of Elizabeth Barrett Browning to her Sister Arabella* (2002).

Focus on: wordplay

ANALYSE . . .

— James Blackadder's footnote says that the name 'Sybilla Silt' is 'an obvious reference to Hella Lees' (p. 299). Why is this? Look up 'lees' and 'silt' in a dictionary if you need to.

ASK YOURSELF . . .

— Val goes through the pile of ephemera by the telephone. It includes a list of flyers advertising 'OMO DAZ KODAK MUREX' (p. 302). One of these is the odd one out. Do you know which? And if you do, do you know what the joke is? If you don't, you will find it in a poem by Robert Browning. Look up the words in a dictionary. Once you have the answer, consider how this teasing reference relates to the themes of the novel as a whole. Use this list to help you:

● Scholarly research
● Clues
● Cross-reference
● Word games

WORK OUT THE PUNS . . .

— Mortimer Cropper walks through Soho and considers whether or not to indulge his 'precise, narrow, and somewhat specialist' tastes in sex (p. 304). The text gives us a quick list of key words drawn from the ads and windows that he passes: 'Peepshow. Model. Young girls wanted. Live Sex NonStop. Come Up and Have Fun. Serious Instruction.' How many puns can you find in this short passage? What is the effect of this list a) on your attitude to Cropper, and b) on the way you are encouraged to imagine the scene?

Focus on: plotting

DRAW A DIAGRAM . . .

— Characters other than Maud and Roland are now becoming interested in the Randolph/Christabel connection. Draw a diagram of which character belongs to which scholarly 'camp'. Then draw a new diagram of how they are beginning to overlap and stray from one to the other. How does this help you to untangle the twentieth-century plot?

CHAPTER EIGHTEEN
(pp. 306–29)

Focus on: clues

MAKE YOURSELF THE DETECTIVE . . .

— Read over this chapter very carefully. There are a number of clues in here that make connections between other events and scenes that you have already come across in the book. Look out for words and phrases, objects and items, colours and names. Imagine that you are now in the position of Roland and Maud, trying to piece together Christabel and

Randolph's story, and see how many clues you can find.

Focus on: landscape and reference

RESEARCH . . .

— On p. 313, you will see the text of Ariane Le Minier's letter to Leonora Stern. You will see that she compliments Stern on an article she is supposed to have written: 'May I say in particular how very just and inspiring I found your remarks on the sexualisation of the landscape elements in *The Fairy Melusina*.' There are a number of scholarly articles on various elements of Victorian literature that take this kind of theme, but you might like to look at Isobel Armstrong's article on Robert Browning in her book *Language as Living Form* (1982). Then consider how and in what way a landscape may be 'sexualised'. Would it be to do with shapes or geographies that might imply body parts? Or with images that might suggest reproductive functions – whether female or male? When you've thought about this, look back at the extract on pp. 289–98 which is from LaMotte's *The Fairy Melusina* and see how many 'sexualised' images you can find in the landscape setting for the poem.

CHAPTER NINETEEN
(pp. 330–82)

Focus on: repetition and difference

EXAMINE AND ASSESS . . .

In the extract from LaMotte's *The City of Is* that opens this chapter, Byatt uses a ballad form where the story builds through question and answer, and repetition and difference.

— Look over the poem and work out where the differences

and the similarities lie. Then ask yourself how any one of these themes listed below may be played out, a) in the poem extract itself, and b) in the novel as a whole.

- Repetition
- Survival
- Rescue
- Resolution

— Read on to the next brief section where Roland and Maud are travelling by boat to France (pp. 332–3). What parallels can you make between the story in the poem and what is happening to Roland and Maud in this passage? If you don't remember right away, look back to see what is special about the magical city of Is.

Focus on: wordplay and mixed metaphors

SEEK OUT AND CONSIDER . . .

— Look at some of these phrases drawn from pp. 332–5: 'this giddy clear-headedness' (p. 332); 'the dark beyond the pale' (p. 333); 'Everything was absurd and at one' (p. 333); 'Roland lay peacefully on his inferior bunk' (p. 333); 'as she moved above him' (p.333); 'to the end of the earth, to Finistère' (p. 335). How many of these phrases include contradiction, mixed images, puns, or double meanings? Why might wordplay of this kind be appropriate to this particular novel?

— Then look again at Roland and Maud's discussion on p. 333. Roland is 'perfectly aware of the absurd range of this comment between mythography, sexual preference and distribution of bolted bunks'. A little bit further down Roland thinks about Michelet and 'the phosphorescent semen of herrings which Michelet, mixing his genders and functions as he had a habit of doing, called the sea of milk, *la mer de lait'*. Over the page, Ariane and Maud discuss 'liminality' (things on borders or margins, or crossing over from one state to another) and the 'transitional area'. Again, ask yourself why mixed metaphors and many layered or multiple images might be an appropriate method for this particular novel.

Focus on: 'narrative greed'

ASK YOURSELF . . .
— Who – inside and outside this novel – experiences 'narrative greed' (p. 335)? Might this phrase include you – the reader? And in what ways does your experience of reading *Possession* compare with Roland and Maud's experience of 'reading' Christabel and Randolph's romance? Remember too that the subtitle of the novel is 'A Romance'.

Focus on: Sabine

ASSESS AND TRANSFORM . . .
— Consider the things that you learn about Sabine from these pages of her journal (pp. 333–79). Then write a short story of about one side as if it were written by Sabine herself. Use her literary techniques and interests. In what ways does Sabine help you to assess what you know of Christabel's character?

Focus on: metaphors

LOOK UP AND CONSIDER . . .
— Look up the word 'metaphor' in the glossary or a dictionary of literary terms. Sabine says that she is 'making metaphors' (p. 339). Work out which these are and how they work. Then look at the interview (p. 25) with Byatt where she speaks of metaphors and their importance in our ways of thinking. Why is the image or metaphor so important to the novel as a whole?

CONSIDER . . .
— Read this passage from pp. 339–40.

> I have much to learn about the organisation of my
> discourse. I wanted, when I was writing about my
> father's bed, both to describe my mother's bed,
> which followed on, and to construct a disquisition or
> digression on box-beds and the borderland between
> fact and fancy which also followed on. I have not
> been wholly successful – there are awkward gaps and
> hops in the sequence, like too-great holes in the dry-
> stone wall. But something is done, and how *inter-
> esting* it all is, seen as craftwork which can be
> bettered, or remade, or scrapped as an apprentice
> piece.

— Think about the ideas that Sabine expresses here and consider how relevant they might be to the narrative of *Possession*
as a whole. Note particularly these words:

- Digression
- Borderland
- Gaps
- Craftwork

Focus on: the fallen woman

CONTRAST AND COMPARE . . .
— Look at the section where Sabine tells Christabel the story
of the old customs of the village girls (pp. 351–2). Then look
at the story that Gode tells on pp. 356–62. Consider the one
in the light of the other. What does the comparison suggest?
Why do you suppose Christabel is so interested? You will note
that on p. 351 Christabel worries about the village girl who is

'stoned' by the others. Sabine corrects her. But what might Christabel be thinking? A clue: look up Jesus's statement, 'He that is without sin among you, let him first cast a stone', and assess what you find in the light of these episodes.

Focus on: Sabine and her father

CONSIDER AND RESEARCH . . .

— In this section, Sabine resents Christabel's presence and, in particular, she regrets the growing intellectual intimacy between the two older people. Work out what Sabine's attitudes to her father might be. Jot down ten key words that might describe the relationship. At the end of this chapter Ariane's letter to Maud briefly tells what happened to Sabine. How does this tale connect to her feelings about her father? Then think about other fathers in this novel as a whole and make as many links as you can between them. When you get to the very end of the novel you might like to reconsider this question.

Focus on: spiritualism

MAKE CONNECTIONS . . .

— Throughout the novel so far there have been occasional scattered references to spiritualism and the work of mediums. Look back over your reading and find those instances. How much information do you have about this by now? Make a note of each episode and consider how each one may relate to others so far. Then – if you have not yet read to the end of the book – ask yourself how this strand might be about to be developed.

Focus on: images and metaphors

CONTEMPLATE . . .

— Sabine thinks of Christabel as a serpent (p. 366). Where have you met the 'serpent' image before in the novel?

BRAINSTORM . . .
— How many associations can you come up with that go with the idea of the serpent or the snake? Use a dictionary of symbolism to help you.

RESEARCH . . .
— Look up any or all of these mythological figures, using a dictionary of mythology or the Internet:

● Lamia
● Medusa
● Eve

— How do they help to focus Byatt's treatment of the image of the serpent in the novel as a whole?

Focus on: romance

MAKE LINKS . . .
— The subtitle of *Possession* is 'A Romance'. Look at Christabel's remarks about romance on p. 373. How does this passage help you to assess the relevance of the subtitle? Byatt discusses this in the interview (pp. 11–12).

Focus on: whiteness

MAKE A NOTE . . .
— In the draft manuscript poem by Christabel that appears on pp. 381–2 there are several references to whiteness. Begin by looking over the whole of Sabine's journal to see how many other allusions to whiteness are included there. Note them down.

BRAINSTORM . . .
— How many associations can you think of that go with the colour white? Here is a list to help you, but work out why they

make you think about 'white' and add as many of your own as you can.

- Purity
- Invisibility
- Brides
- Death
- Blanks

ASSESS THE IMAGE . . .
— Ask yourself how many instances of 'whiteness' you have met in the novel so far. Make another list. How and where is this image used in the novel as a whole?

CHAPTER TWENTY
(pp. 383–404)

Focus on: the cabinet of curiosities

CONNECT . . .
— Cropper gives his lecture, complete with slides and holograms of precious items associated with Randolph Henry Ash (pp. 385–7). Look back over the exercises on the idea of the cabinet of curiosities and the image of the museum (Chapters Two and Six). This passage will give you connections to those. What kind of story can you build up about this image of the precious object across the novel as a whole?

Focus on: spiritualism

ASSESS . . .
— On pp. 387–9 we are given Christabel's letter to Mortimer

Cropper's ancestor. Work out how this might go with the episodes we have already seen that deal with spiritualism and Christabel's interest in mediums and their skills.

Focus on: narrative styles

DISCRIMINATE . . .

— Look over this chapter and note down the various different styles of narrative. How many can you find? Remember to include the 'soundbite' television appearances of Blackadder and Leonora Stern towards the end of the chapter. When you have as many different items on your list as you can find, think how many other narrative styles you have seen so far in the novel. Then think about how the question of narrative method is used as a theme, or as an image, or as a subject of discussion in the novel as a whole. Think also about the places where 'narrative greed' or ways of storytelling are discussed in the novel overall.

Focus on: allusion and Randolph's 'Gaza exploit'

GUESS OR RESEARCH THE REFERENCE . . .

— Why does Randolph Henry Ash call this his 'Gaza exploit'? Work out the biblical figure to which this refers and the specific actions of that character which may provide – and clearly do in Randolph's mind – a parallel with what happens at Hella Lees seance. If you look at the paragraph on pp. 390–1 beginning 'I am convinced as I may be that we are all being practised upon', you will find a clue about pulling down 'the house of cards'.

Focus on: allusion and vocabulary

RESEARCH . . .

— There are two words repeated many times in various different settings in these passages: they are 'odylic' and 'actinic'.

Look both these words up in the *Oxford English Dictionary* and consider their function here. They are both arcane and unusual words. What is the effect of that strangeness on your attitude as a reader?

ASK YOURSELF . . .
— The spirit invoked by Hella Lees says 'Remember the stones' (p. 396) and 'Whose were the stones?' (p. 397). Do you know the answer from your own reading of the novel so far? What (real) stones may these be? And what (metaphoric) significance might they have? If you can't work it out immediately, look back at pp. 287, 308 and 351 to make the connections.

Focus on: irony

ASK HOW AND WHY? . . .
— Leonora Stern and James Blackadder appear on a television programme called *Events in Depth*. Why is this an ironic title, especially given how much we know about the Christabel and Randolph story so far? And why is it ironic that it ends up being Blackadder and Stern that appear on the television programme?

CHAPTER TWENTY-ONE
(pp. 405–12)

Focus on: poetry

RESEARCH AND COMPARE . . .
— Read Robert Browning's narrative poem 'Mr Sludge, "the Medium"' for a comparison with Ash's supposed poem *Mummy Possest*. Then look at the beginning (at least) of Browning's early poem *Sordello* which has an opening similar to that

given here for Ash. You might also like to look at Samuel Taylor Coleridge's 'Christabel' for another source of comparison (the other major character in Coleridge's poem is called 'Geraldine').

CHAPTER TWENTY-TWO
(pp. 413–17)

Focus on: plotting

WORK OUT . . .

— Think about the ways in which the plot is being moved on here. Why is it important that Toby and Euan become involved? How do you feel about Val's part in this and in what will happen to her now? Further on, at p. 498, Maud will say, 'We need the end of the story.' Do you find that you need the end of Val's story too?

CHAPTER TWENTY-THREE
(pp. 418–29)

Focus on: vocabulary and wordplay

EXAMINE AND ASSESS THE RELEVANCE . . .

— This chapter begins with a word game on page 418 – 'The irruption, or interruption'. It goes on to play with the word 'trespass' and the word '*sein*' – breast or womb in French. How do these episodes – and this juxtaposition of Maud and Roland with Leonora and James – connect to the themes of the novel as a whole?

LOOK AHEAD . . .
— On p. 423, in the paragraph beginning 'Things had changed
between them nevertheless', there is a list of theoretical and
technical critical terms. Look up some or all of these. What is
the effect of this list here? How does it draw attention to words
and wordplay? Does it matter that you may not know – without
looking them up – what all the words mean?

Focus on: narrative greed

INTERPRET . . .
— 'Roland thought, partly with precise postmodernist
pleasure, and partly with a real element of superstitious dread,
that he and Maud were being driven by a plot or fate that
seemed, at least possibly, to be not their plot or fate but that
of those others' (p. 421). Consider and interpret this remark in
the light of a) the fact that this is a novel, and b) the fact that
these are scholars unravelling a story. Look through the rest of
this complex paragraph to see how the continuing analysis
might help you.

Focus on: the fallen woman

COMPARE . . .
— Look out some or all of the references that are included in
Maud's list on p. 422: the character of Gretchen is in Goethe's
Faust; Hetty Sorrel appears in George Eliot's *Adam Bede*; Martha
is in William Wordworth's poem 'The Thorn'. How do any of
these comparative figures help you to contemplate Christabel's
reactions and attitudes?

Focus on: genre, and Romance versus Quest

DECIDE . . .
— On p. 425 Roland thinks about the terms of the 'Romance'

form and the terms of the 'Quest'. Find out as much as you can about both of these literary forms. Then put the following list of works (as many as you know, or can find out about) under one or other of the two headings:

- Charlotte Brontë's *Jane Eyre*
- J. K. Rowling's *Harry Potter and the Philosopher's Stone*
- T. H. White's *The Sword in the Stone*
- Daphne du Maurier's *Rebecca*
- Samuel Taylor Coleridge's *The Rime of the Ancient Mariner*
- Michael Curtiz's (1942) film *Casablanca*
- Sebastian Faulks's *Birdsong*
- Steven Spielberg's (1993) film *Jurassic Park*

CHAPTER TWENTY-FOUR
(pp. 430–41)

Focus on: repetition, difference and poetry

CONSIDER AND ANALYSE . . .

— In the opening sections to this chapter there are repetitions and half-memories of phrases and words. Look at the brief account of Maud's notes on p. 430, and at the ways in which the narrative describes Maud and Roland's slightly awkward relationship to one another at this stage. How might this help you to think about what is happening to Roland as he makes his lists of words on p. 431? (There will be some part of an explanation later on at pp. 472–5). For the moment, consider Roland's lists. How might the words in each discrete section be linked? Let your mind wander over the possibilities. Certain key ideas might help, such as: colour, significance, body shapes, reproduction, metamorphosis. When you have written down as much as you can, think over what has happened in the novel so far and see how much of Roland's lists might be linked – however tenuously – to the scenes and the images and themes that you have seen played out there.

Focus on: characterisation

ASK YOURSELF ABOUT ROLAND . . .

— 'Lady Bailey was good to us. She could do with the wheelchair' (p. 437). Roland will say the same thing later on. Why does it matter? How does this help you to come to an assessment of his character and what he values?

CHAPTER TWENTY-FIVE
(pp. 442–62)

Focus on: narrative method

COUNT UP . . .

— As the threads of the story are being pulled together, several different narrative styles and methods, scenes and circumstances are employed here. We make it at least eleven – but you may be able to distinguish more. Our list would include:

● Ellen Ash's journal
● Mortimer Cropper's biography of Ash
● The attendant footnotes
● The third-person narrative telling about Ellen as an old lady after Ash's death
● A letter from Christabel to Ellen – sent, received and read
● Ellen Ash's imagined drafts of letters in reply to Christabel – never written
● A dialogue between Ellen and Randolph, autumn 1859
● A dialogue between Ellen and Blanche

- A draft of a letter from Randolph to Christabel – not sent, burned by Ellen
- A narrative mediated through the omniscient third person, but telling the story of Ellen's honeymoon from her point of view
- A letter from Ash to Ellen written during their courtship – sent, received, read, kept, buried

— When you have completed your list, put the episodes in chronological order. In this case the earliest will be Ash's letter to Ellen written during their courtship, and the latest will be Mortimer Cropper's biography, published in 1967. How does the setting out of this chronological narrative help you to assess the actual published version? Consider the dramatic impact that is created by organising these elements in the order in which they are published. Essentially, we end the chapter with a story about Ellen and Randolph – and we have seen very little of that relation so far. What difference does it make to your perspective on Christabel and Randolph's affair to be given this – rather belated – account of the Ashes' courtship and the early days of their marriage? And what is the effect of the fact that the last words in this chapter are Christabel's?

Focus on: 'the Protean letter'

COMPARE AND CONNECT . . .
— On p. 462, Ellen thinks of her imagined response to Christabel. It is described by a 'Protean letter' – that is, something that constantly changes its form. The reference is to Proteus, a figure in classical mythology who could turn himself into any shape at will. Think about this idea and the way that the letter keeps being revised in Ellen's mind. Then look at the paragraph that includes this reference: 'And the crystalline forms, the granite, the hornblende-schist, shone darkly

with the idea that she would not write, that the Protean letter
would form and reform, in her head, that it might become too
late, too late for decency, absolutely too late.' How does this
paragraph connect to the themes of the novel as a whole?
Consider the image of collections and cabinets of curiosity that
you have traced previously. Consider also the theme of metamorphosis that you have followed throughout.

CHAPTER TWENTY-SIX
(pp. 463–75)

Focus on: the theme of the hidden garden

LOOK BACK . . .
There is a place to which all Poets come
[. . .]
Who chance upon the path in thickest dream,
Some lost in mythy mazes, some direct
From fear of death, or lust of life or thought
And some who lost themselves in Arcady . . . (p. 463).

— If you look back to the extract from Christabel LaMotte's
The Fairy Melusine that we saw on pp. 289–98, and in particular at the episode where the knight finds the mysterious lady
in the wood (pp. 295–6), you will see that that too is set in a
hidden garden. How many such 'gardens' or secret woodland
places have you seen in the novel so far? Include Christabel
and Randolph's visit to the Boggle Hole, include the garden at
Kernemat, and – especially at this point – the garden that is
beyond Roland and Val's basement flat. Make as many connections as you can between all of these gardens that you have
encountered so far. Once you have finished, you will see that
there are at least two more important 'gardens' to come.

CONSIDER GARDENS AND POETRY . . .

— Consider 'garden' poems, especially those that include a moment of poetic reverie that occurs in that garden. There are many poems of this kind: the *Roman de la Rose* by Guillaume de Lorris and Jean de Meun (le Clopinel) is an early (thirteenth century) model, which was partially translated by Chaucer; Sidney's *Arcadia* and Spenser's *The Faerie Queen* are important examples. You might also look at Donne's 'The Ecstasy'; Marvell's 'The Garden'; Coleridge's 'This Lime-Tree Bower my Prison'; Wordsworth's 'She dwelt among the untrodden ways'; Keats's 'Ode to a Nightingale'; Tennyson's 'Mariana'; Hardy's 'The Darkling Thrush'; Yeats's 'The Wild Swans at Coole'; 'Edward Thomas's 'The Bright Field'; and Eleanor Farjeon's 'Easter Morning, 1916'. How does the poetic trope of the moment of bucolic contemplation and literary reverie make sense in relation to the themes of *Possession* as a whole? Look at the paragraph on p. 471 which begins 'Think of this, as Roland thought of it' and which ends 'elastic-walled and grey round blind eyes'. Use this paragraph to help you focus your ideas.

Focus on: vocabulary

REFLECT . . .

— On pp. 470–1, the third-person narrator offers a little aside about the word 'heady'. Given that this is a novel about poetry and poets and writing, words are of paramount importance. In what ways is your own experience of the novel also 'heady'?

Focus on: naming

RELATE . . .

— 'What Ash said . . . was that the lists were the important thing, the words that named things, the language of poetry' (p. 473). How does this quotation help to explain the ways in which the novel works as a whole?

CHAPTER TWENTY-SEVEN
(pp. 476–86)

Focus on: the theme of possession

KEEP A LOOK OUT FOR . . .
— From now on the theme, the word and the idea of different forms of 'possession' keep recurring. Look out for all of these references and note the different ways in which the idea is used as the novel pulls all its threads together.

Focus on: the cabinet of curiosities

NOTE AND COMPARE . . .
— On p. 484, Blackadder suggests that Cropper might have collected for himself 'a private, inaccessible inner cabinet of curios that he turns over, and breathes in at the dead of night, things no one ever sees'. In what ways does the idea of the cabinet of precious items that is never seen connect to the scenes and events that you have read in the novel so far?

CHAPTER TWENTY-EIGHT
(pp. 487–507)

Focus on: literary genre and the detective novel

DISTINGUISH THE CONSTITUENTS . . .
— Throughout the novel we have been encouraged to consider narratives and methods of storytelling, poetic connection and ways of organising discourse. Here, in the (almost) last chapter, one last form is brought clearly to the fore – though it has been hinted at in the idea of the search and the hunt for clues. This is the form of the conventional detective story. Work out the ways in which this form is now being parodied.

Write yourself a list of the elements that usually appear in the classic detective novel. One way of doing this would be to look at some of these. You could try Wilkie Collins's *The Moonstone* (1868), Conan Doyle's *The Hound of the Baskervilles* (1902), Agatha Christie's *Murder on the Orient Express* (1934), Barbara Vine's *A Fatal Inversion* (1987) or P. D. James's *Original Sin* (1994). Another route into this might be to look at a pastiche of the classic detective novel, simply because it will set out the key terms and constituents in a clearly designated way. A good example of this genre would be Tom Stoppard's play *The Real Inspector Hound* (1968). You might even think about the terms that are built into the popular board game Cluedo. Some of the constituents might include: the country house (or a luxury train, as in the case of *Murder on the Orient Express*); a restricted group of diverse characters; the group cut off from the world, for whatever emergency reason, creating some unsettling of class or status or role in terms of dress or behaviour or disguise; the question of who did what, with what, to whom, and where. Note that: Euan says to Cropper, 'You're surrounded' (p. 496). Then he says, 'I've *always* wanted to say "You are surrounded"' (p. 497). In what ways does this indicate that Byatt is consciously reworking the detective-novel form?

Focus on: the dragon and its allusions

RELATE . . .
— In the course of the novel so far we have met many 'dragons', 'serpents' and 'Lamias'. Now, on p. 492, the narrative says, 'Above the owl, the dragon moved a little, this way, that way, creaking, desisting, catching a desultory air movement.' Shortly, you will find out what this natural phenomenon might be, but for now, treat the image as a poetic symbol and look back to work out how many 'dragon' connections you can make overall. Remember to include the dressing gown that Maud wears while

staying with the Baileys, and remember to look closely at both Christabel's and Randolph's poems.

— Once you have done that, look over this chapter and seek out as many references as you can to dragons, serpents and snakes. Include personifications in the natural world. Finally, reconsider all the mythological references to dragons and serpents that you have accumulated. These will include: Proserpina and the golden apples, Eve, Ladon, Medusa, Lamia, Melusina. All the metaphoric connections that you make are important and relevant. You are telling a story about a story.

Focus on: the theme of the hidden garden

INVESTIGATE . . .

— Roland and Maud 'sat side by side on the edge of a four-poster bed, hung about with William Morris golden lilies' (p. 504). Find out about William Morris's fabric and wallpaper designs. There are a number of books on the subject, and collections in the Victoria and Albert Museum, at Kelmscott Manor in Oxfordshire and at Wightwick Manor in Wolverhampton. 'Golden lilies' is a design not by Morris himself, but by one of his disciples, but it is still produced today, as many of his designs are, by Sanderson and by Liberty. How does this image relate to the idea of the hidden garden that has run throughout the novel? And why is it important that Roland and Maud should meet in a 'garden' of some kind?

LINK AND SHAPE . . .

— Think again about Randolph and Christabel in the hotel by the sea. On p. 279 we were told that their dinner was served on plates 'rimmed with cobalt blue and spattered with fat pink rosebuds'. On p. 282 we saw that their bedroom was 'papered with trellises of monstrous roses on a cabbage-green ground'. We are also told the words that they speak to each other: She:

91

'Are you afraid?' and he: 'Not in the least, now' (p. 283). Take these two elements in these episodes from different parts of the book and make as many links as you can. You too will be making a narrative shape, just as the characters in this novel do, just as the novel itself does (and yours will be no less than the others).

POSTSCRIPT 1868
(pp. 508–11)

Focus on: 'narrative greed'

CONTEMPLATE . . .

— The third-person narrator appears here – a rare appearance in the novel. Byatt refers to this in the interview (pp. 20–21). The narrative tells us that this is because 'There are things which happen and leave no discernible trace, are not spoken or written of, though it would be very wrong to say that subsequent events go on indifferently, all the same, as though such things had never been' (p. 508). Is this a satisfactory end to the story? We had thought that it was Ash who was left 'not knowing' at the end of the twentieth-century story. Now we find that he did know, and that it was Christabel LaMotte who lived with 'not knowing' that he knew. How does this make you feel? What are your reactions to the giving or withholding of knowledge, both for you and for the characters in the novel? Is your own 'narrative greed' satisfied?

Focus on: the hidden garden

COMPARE . . .

— Byatt says in the interview (p. 20 and pp. 30–1) that she cannot resist the temptation to end her novels with a reference to John Milton's *Paradise Lost*. Look at what she says there, and compare those remarks with the events and settings of *Possession*. If you have read Byatt's *A Whistling Woman*, you might also like to compare the ending of that novel with the ending of this.

Focus on: poetry

RELATE . . .
— There are several references to English poetry in this Postscript, including an allusion to Milton's *Lycidas*, to Keats's 'La Belle Dame Sans Merci' and to the poems that we have read during the course of the novel. Look up any of these poems, inside and outside the text, and consider how they might reflect on each other.

Focus on: endings

ASK YOURSELF . . .
— 'The lovely crown was broken, and she forgot the message, which never was delivered' (p. 511). In what ways is this an appropriate ending for this novel?

Looking over the whole novel

QUESTIONS FOR DISCUSSION OR ESSAYS
1. Consider the importance of ANY ONE OR TWO of these minor characters in the unfolding of the plot or the themes of *Possession*:

● Ellen Ash
● Beatrice Nest
● Sabine de Kercoz
● Leonora Stern
● George Bailey
● Joan Bailey
● Val

2. Analyse the importance of naming as a theme in *Possession*.

3. Explain and justify the subtitle of the novel, 'A Romance'.

4. Consider the theme of 'possession' in the novel.

5. 'How true it was that one needed to be seen by others to be sure of one's own existence' (p. 468). Consider the ways in which this statement relates to the themes of the novel as a whole.

6. 'We need the end of the story' (p. 498). Discuss the imperatives of narrative in *Possession*.

7. Explore the idea of 'Victorian Doubt' in *Possession*.

8. Discuss the representation of cyclical time in *Possession*.

9. Consider the representation of the Victorian past and its effects on the present in *Possession*.

10. Examine the use of the enclosed space in Byatt's setting in *Possession*.

11. Discuss Byatt's use of literary mimicry in *Possession*.

12. What is the significance of the novel's title?

13. Assess whether the poems are a necessary and integral part of the novel or would it have worked just as well without them?

14. How do Byatt's choices of names help define the relationships between the characters?

15. In what ways do Ash's and LaMotte's diction and subject matter fulfil ideas of 'masculine' and 'feminine' poetry?

16. Consider the novel's treatment of the line between a ghoulish intrusion upon the privacy of the dead, and the legitimate claims of scholarship and history.

17. Consider the importance of freedom and autonomy to Christabel and to Maud, paying attention to the different social pressures that constrain them.

18. 'Beatrice Nest is as much a victim of "patriarchy" as any of the Victorian women studied by the scholars in the novel.' Discuss.

19. Apart from the quest that they believe they are taking part in, what other elements of Romance can be found in Maud and Roland's story?

Contexts, comparisons and complementary readings

These sections suggest contextual and comparative ways of reading the three novels by Byatt. You can put your reading in a social, historical or literary context. You can make comparisons – again, social, literary or historical – with other texts or art works. Or you can choose complementary works (of whatever kind) – that is, art works, literary works, social reportage or facts which in some way illuminate the text by sidelights or interventions which you can make into a telling framework. Some of the suggested contexts are directly connected to the book, in that they will give you precise literary or social frames in which to situate the novel. In turn, these are either related to the period within which the novel is set, or to the time – now – when you are reading it. Some of these examples are designed to suggest books or other texts that may make useful sources for comparison (or for complementary purposes) when you are reading *Possession, Angels & Insects* and *A Whistling Woman*. Again, they may be related to literary or critical themes, or they may be relevant to social and cultural themes current 'then' or 'now'.

Focus on: libraries

RESEARCH . . .

— At the beginning of the book, Roland is in the London Library, a private library founded in the nineteenth century and established in St James's Square in London. Members have to pay a subscription and may borrow books as well as using the reference and manuscript sections. What do you think libraries are for? What different kinds of library are there? As you work through the book, make a note of all the libraries you find. These will include: the London library, Dr Williams's Library, the British Library (when it was in the British Museum – it is now housed on a new site at St Pancras), the Stant Collection, the Women's Studies resource centre in Lincoln, Maud's own library, Roland's library and Ash's library. There are others.

— By the end, there is something discovered – in the box in the Ash tomb – that is not in a library. Of all the libraries and collections you have seen in the course of the novel, which do you consider the most suitable home for the contents of this box? Or should it – in your opinion – be put back into the tomb?

Focus on: letters

CONTRAST AND COMPARE . . .

— This is the beginning of the first letter that Robert Browning wrote to Elizabeth Barrett in January 1845.

> I love your verses with all my heart, dear Miss
> Barrett – and this is no off-hand complimentary
> letter that I shall write . . . since the day last week

when I first read your poems, I quite laugh to
remember how I have been turning and turning
again in my mind, what I should be able to tell you
of their effect upon me . . .

How does it compare with the drafts of Randolph's letter to
Christabel?

Focus on: Victorian poetry

CONTRAST AND COMPARE . . .
— Byatt made up the poems attributed to Christabel and to
Ash. Find a collection of poems by Christina Rossetti and a
collection of poems by Emily Dickinson, and compare their
work with the invented parodies of Christabel's work composed
by Byatt.

Focus on: literary influence

CONSIDER . . .
— On p. 265, Roland remarks that LaMotte's *The Fairy
Melusina* is very like Ash's work, and that it is almost as though
he might have written it. Maud does not wish this to be so,
but agrees on the similarity. In the early twentieth-century a
poem by Elizabeth Barrett called 'Aeschylus's Soliloqy' was mis-
takenly attributed to her husband Robert Browning. What does
this suggest about literary influences?

Focus on: blondes

CONSIDER THE IMPLICATIONS . . .

— In the interview (p. 15) Byatt speaks about blondes and colour-coding. With what do you associate blondeness? Think of portraits of the Madonna and of Mary Magdalene – which one is most frequently portrayed as blonde? Look at George Eliot's novel *The Mill on the Floss*. Maggie is dark, Lucy is blonde – Maggie has something to say about this and how the blonde girl always gets the man in the end.

THINK ABOUT THESE QUOTATIONS . . .

- 'Gentlemen prefer blondes' (Anita Loos).
- 'It was a blonde. A blonde to make a bishop kick a hole in a stained-glass window' (Raymond Chandler).

— What do they suggest about blondes?

RESEARCH . . .

— Look out Marina Warner's book *From the Beast to the Blonde: Fairy Tales and their Tellers* (1996). This will help you to focus your theoretical ideas about colour-coding and dark and blonde.

Focus on: ventriloquism

RESEARCH AND APPLY . . .

— 'Ventriloquism' means all the various forms taken by source-less, displaced and dissociated voices. Refer to instances of ventriloquism throughout literary history: the Greek and Roman oracles, such as the Pythian oracle at Delphi and that of the sibyl at Cumae; myths of the dissociated voice, such as the myth of Orpheus, or that of Echo, who, deprived of a voice of her own in which to express her love for Narcissus, dwindled away until only her voice was left.

— Ventriloquism emerged as a form of popular entertainment only during the nineteenth century. It was linked to the fascination with mediated or manipulated voices in mid-nineteenth-century mesmerism and late-nineteenth-century spiritualism, as well as to the development of technologies for synthesising, reproducing and transforming the voice, and developed into what has become the traditional ventriloquial form of the dialogue with the alter-ego dummy.

— Refer to *Wieland* and *Carwin the Biloquist* by Charles Brockden Brown (1771–1810) for rare instances of the genre of the 'ventriloquist novel'.

Focus on: the wolf figure in fairy tales

READ AND COMPARE . . .

— The best-known fairy tale involving a wolf is *Little Red Riding Hood* (part of the oral tradition, first published in 1697). The version most children know nowadays – in which the little girl and her grandmother are rescued by a huntsman – is a reworking of the original story by the brothers Grimm. Earlier versions show a little girl who is quite able to outwit the wolf herself by performing a striptease and then tricking him into letting her go outside to pee (in some she kills the wolf and ends the story by feasting on his leftovers); other early versions finish with the wolf leaping on the girl and devouring her. Most early forms of the story therefore contain an erotic element that has been expunged from later children's versions. For contemporary reworkings of the theme, refer to James Thurber's *The Little Girl and the Wolf* or to Roald Dahl's *Little Red Riding*

Hood and the Wolf, both of which put the girl back on top (in Dahl she whips a pistol from her knickers and soon sports a 'lovely furry wolf skin coat'). For cinematic adaptations, watch Neil Jordan's *The Company of Wolves* (1984), based on Angela Carter's novel, or Matthew Bright's *Freeway* (1996). These both explore the erotic possibilities of the story. What use has Byatt made of the erotic dimensions of the wolf figure in *Possession*?

Focus on: fairy tales

RESEARCH THE ALLUSIONS . . .
— If you wish to investigate the numerous allusions to fairy tales in *Possession*, you might refer to *The Annotated Classic Fairy Tales*, edited by Maria Tartar (2003).

Focus on: names

RESEARCH . . .
— To look up the etymology of any of the names used in *Possession*, or any other text for that matter, you might refer to the website http://www.behindthename.com, which also allows you to research names in literature.

Focus on: Darwin and doubt

CONSIDER THE PARALLELS . . .
— 'Doubt,' says Christabel, 'doubt is endemic to our life in this world at this time'. The year 1859, the moment of crisis in the poets' lives, was an especially significant year because it saw

the publication of Charles Darwin's *On the Origin of Species*. This work undermined the Victorians' faith in the idea of man as God's supreme creation, and created a climate of uncertainty. Consider how Byatt compares this spiritual crisis with that which has befallen Roland and Maud's generation, who are taught to believe that the 'self' is illusory (p. 459).

Focus on: Byatt's official website

RESEARCH . . .
— Visit Byatt's official website, which is under development, at http://www.asbyatt.com. It includes an essay by Byatt on the writing of *Possession*.

Focus on: film adaptation

COMPARE MEDIA . . .
— Adapting *Possession*, which is about the power of words, into a film presents particular problems, such as how to portray the use of correspondence, diaries, and verse. Screenwriters David Henry Hwang and Laura Jones adapted the novel for a film by director Neil LaBute (2002). 'LaBute's examination of the way sexual mores shift over the centuries never becomes more than superficial, a surprising flaw given his past work. For a film that depends so much on the interaction between words and passion – and the drama of how each shapes the other – the shortage of both leaves *Possession* looking like nothing more than an *Indiana Jones* in which card catalogues stand in for treasure maps, and footnotes for bullwhips'. Watch the film and assess how successfully it translates the novel's concerns to the screen.

Focus on: further reading on the Victorian period

RESEARCH . . .

— Much of the background to *Possession* is based in a very careful study of the motives and interests of the nineteenth century. If you are interested in researching this area, then some of these books may be useful to you:

- Jerome H. Buckley, *The Victorian Temper*
- Frank Kermode, *Romantic Image*
- Robert Langbaum, *The Poetry of Experience*
- Phyllis Rose, *Parallel Lives*
- Lionel Stevenson, *Darwin Among the Poets*

Focus on: the modern novel that plays with the past

LOOK OUT FOR . . .

— *Possession* is a modern novel – even though part of its story is set in the past. This is a technique adopted by other novelists too, and you might like to compare some of these suggested novels with Byatt's *Possession*:

- Julian Barnes, *Flaubert's Parrot*
- Anthony Burgess, *Nothing Like the Sun*
- Italo Calvino, *The Baron in the Trees*
- Italo Calvino, *The Castle of Crossed Destinies*
- Umberto Eco, *The Name of the Rose*
- John Fowles, *The Ebony Tower*
- John Fowles, *The French Lieutenant's Woman*
- Iris Murdoch, *The Black Prince*
- Iris Murdoch, *The Philosopher's Pupil*

VINTAGE
LIVING
TEXTS

Angels & Insects

IN CLOSE-UP

Reading guides for

ANGELS & INSECTS

BEFORE YOU BEGIN TO READ . . .
— Read the interview with Byatt. You will see there that she identifies a number of themes and techniques:

- Metamorphosis and Butterflies
- Metaphor
- Colour
- Darwinian selection
- Wordplay
- Poetry

Other themes that may be useful to consider while reading the novel include:

- Exploration
- Fairy tales and Storytelling
- Freedom
- Order and disorder
- Spiritualism
- Love

Reading activities: detailed analysis

Focus on: the title

JUXTAPOSE . . .
— Make as many connections as you can between 'angels' and 'insects'. Why is this a surprising pairing? Think about the ways in which they are similar (do they both have wings, for instance?) and then think about the ways in which they are different: one is eternal, the other ephemeral, for example. Once you have compiled your list, keep it by you as you read and consult it occasionally to see how those circumstances and images might apply to the events and themes that unfold in the two stories included here.

CONSIDER . . .
— You are going to read two long short stories, or two novellas, in this book. Each has a different title, and yet they are both linked under this collective title of *Angels & Insects*. While you are reading – but especially once you have come to the end of both stories – consider how this overall title is used in relation to each story and how the two stories are connected.

Focus on: the pleasure of reading

ANALYSE . . .
— In Byatt's *Possession*, there is a section in Chapter Twenty-Six (pp. 470–2 in the Vintage edition) where the omniscient third-person narrator tells us about Roland reading poetry and how that may be an intense pleasure. Consider the ways in which the task of making connections and comparisons across these two stories may be similarly pleasurable. Use some of these key words to help you:

- Recognition
- Comparison
- Difference
- Contrast
- Parallels

'MORPHO EUGENIA'

Focus on: the title

LOOK OUT FOR . . .
— Morpho Eugenia is a kind of butterfly. Look out for points in the text where the name and its significance are discussed by the characters (such as on pp. 20–1), and refer to what Byatt says about it in the interview.

SECTION I
(pp. 3–8)

Focus on: colour

DISCRIMINATE . . .

— Consider the ways in which colour is used in this section. There are the colours of the dresses the various girls are wearing, but there is also some discussion of the Alabaster family's hereditary colouring, and of the hierarchy of difference in skin colouring, whether in this ballroom, or in the Amazon. If you have read *Possession* you will know that Byatt uses colour to hint at connections and thematic resonances. She says something about this in the interview (pp. 14–16). Remember the use of colour in this opening passage – we shall come back to it.

Focus on: naming

CONSIDER THE CONNOTATIONS . . .

— What does it suggest to you that the family is called 'Alabaster'? What does it suggest to you that William is called 'Adamson'? Byatt chooses her characters' names carefully for their associations and allusions. To look up the etymology of any of the names used, you might refer to the website http://www.behindthename.com, which also allows you to research names in literature. You might also refer to what Byatt says about naming in the interview (pp. 16–17).

Focus on: fairy tales

NOTE . . .

— Enid and William hold a conversation about the story of the twelve dancing princesses (p. 5). Look up the story if you don't know it already. An Internet search will take you to it.

This is the first of many references and allusions to fairy tales that are scattered throughout the text. Keep a note of such references, so that you can put them together to make a pattern through the text.

Focus on: sex, and sexual selection

ASSESS . . .
Note that a key theme is introduced here as William tells Eugenia that the male butterfly is the one who is gaily coloured, not the female (p. 7). This is, for the most part, the case throughout the natural world: think of the male peacock, or the male lion. 'Morpho Eugenia' is set in the years immediately following the publication of Charles Darwin's influential *On the Origin of Species* (1859). His observations gave a name to two important ideas that governed the process of evolution: sexual selection and natural selection. Sexual selection is to do with the way in which the female of the species chooses the best, most fitting mate, given her particular reproductive circumstances, the introduction of new genes to strengthen the stock of her offspring being one (unconscious) element in that choice. Natural selection denotes the way a species evolves and adapts to its circumstances (habitat, food stocks, necessary physical adaptations or skills). This partly involves sexual selection and partly relies on what is generally called 'the survival of the fittest'; that is, that member of the species who has adapted most successfully to his or her circumstances is the one – assuming the circumstances remain the same – whose genes will survive. Darwinian theory will become an important theme in the novel. You need know no more than is set out in the story itself, but if you are interested in reading Darwin, then there is a helpful annotated edition by Philip Appleman (1975).

SECTION 2
(pp. 8–14)

Focus on: characterisation

MAKE A LIST AND CONSIDER . . .
— Think about William's character as it is revealed in this section. List the elements that make up his distinct personality. You might include the facts of his background, his pleasure in collecting and in cataloguing, his interest in poetry (there is a reference to Wordsworth on p. 10 as well as the quotation from Ben Jonson on p. 12) and in stories. There is also the fact of his telling his own story by keeping a journal. Consider which of these might be the most important key to his character. On pp. 13–14, an extract from his diary attempts to account for the pull he feels between romance and rationality. From the information you have here, try to account for his desire for Eugenia.

SECTION 3
(pp. 14–21)

Focus on: insects

ANALYSE THE ANALOGY . . .
— Note all the references you can find to insects. What kinds of comparison and analogy are being made here? What is suggested by the name of the Alabasters' house, Bredely Hall?

Focus on: colour

CONTINUE MAKING NOTES . . .
— Keep noticing all the references to colour in this section. You will need these notes later on.

Focus on: dialogue

CONTRAST AND ANALYSE . . .
— Look at the speeches that William makes on pp. 16–17 and
18. Then compare the way that he speaks with Harald Alabaster's
speech on pp. 17–18. How do their speeches reveal differences
in their characters?

Focus on: the theme of order and disorder

COMPILE AND REFLECT . . .
On p. 21 there is some discussion between William, Harald
and Eugenia about the name of the butterfly 'Morpho Eugenia'.
This is, of course, also the title of the story overall. Here, we
are told the Latin meaning of 'morpho' – that is 'beautiful', or,
more precisely, 'shapely'. Eugenia notes that this is the Latin
root from which the English word 'amorphous' derives. 'A' is
a negative in Latin, signifying 'not'. 'Amorphous' therefore
means 'not shapely'. In many ways this is a story concerned
with 'shapeliness', both with the perceiving of order or 'shapeliness' in the natural world, and with the various ways in which
one can make order or shapeliness in terms of cataloguing, cat-
egorising, labelling, observing and analysing. These are all scientific modes of 'naming' or 'shaping' our experience of the
world, but storytelling of all kinds is another way of doing that
same thing.
— As you read on, look for the different methods of making
shapes that are in this story. Make a list both of the scientific
techniques and the narrative techniques, such as journals, fairy
tales, allusions, fiction, argument and polemic. As you collect
these examples, consider how telling a story about something
with a view to making an 'order' may also be undermined when
that story is revealed to be false.

SECTION 4
(pp. 21–36)

Focus on: the theme of fairy tale

NOTE . . .

— This section opens with William thinking of himself as a prince in a fairy tale. Remember to make a note of all such references, so as to trace a pattern running through the story.

Focus on: naming and 'race'

INTERPRET . . .

— On p. 22, we are told that Bredely Hall was built 'like a medieval manor house'. Further on, we are given the names of some of the members of the Alabaster family, including Harald, Robert, Joanna, Edgar, Lionel, Gertrude, Margaret, Elaine, Edith, Guy and Alice. We already know that the three daughters of the family are called Eugenia, Rowena and Enid. What kinds of names do you imagine these to be? To what period in history might they belong? Look out a copy of Sir Walter Scott's *Ivanhoe* or Alfred Tennyson's *Idylls of the King* for clues. Then consider what the implications may be of the fact that William's name is . . . William.

— While the Alabaster family are one set of characters introduced here, there is a subset of characters who are the 'poor relations' or who are in the domestic employ of the Alabasters. These include Miss Fescue, Matilda Crompton, the governess Miss Mead and the nursery nurse Dacres (p. 22). What do any or all of these names suggest? Look them up in a dictionary if you do not have ideas right away. (You could try inserting an apostrophe into 'Dacres' to get an appropriate English word.) How do any or all of these names help you to reflect on the theme of the natural world as played out in the novel as a whole?

Focus on: characterisation

ANALYSE AND DESCRIBE . . .

— Look at the description of Lady Alabaster on pp. 26–8 and the account of William's conversation with her. Jot down five key words to describe her character. How is she portrayed? If she were an insect – and this is a major theme of the novel – what kind of an insect might she be? If you don't immediately have an answer for this, wait and think about it later on.

Focus on: nature and theories of evolution

CONNECT . . .

— William's naturalist expeditions with Miss Matty, with the children and (sometimes) with Eugenia are described on pp. 28–32. This is followed with an account of one of William's conversations with Harald (pp. 33–6). Makes as many links as you can between these two episodes. How might the one illuminate the other?

Focus on: Paradise

COMPARE . . .

— There are several references on pp. 29–32 to Paradise – whether that figuring in John Milton's famous poem *Paradise Lost*, or the literary convention of the 'Golden Age', or the biblical story of Creation found in the Book of Genesis in the Old Testament. Consider any tales of Paradise or creation that you know of. What elements usually appear? You might look at this section to add in some of those constituents.

SECTION 5
(pp. 36–44)

Focus on: Queens

INTERPRET THE ANALOGY . . .
— Miss Matty, William and the children in the nursery build a glass hive for the bees and a formicary for the ants. Look over the description of the function of the Queen in each case. Of what might the terms of their existence remind you? You will need to come back to this question later on in the story.

CONTRAST AND COMPARE . . .
— Consider ANY ONE OR MORE of the items listed here. How do the ideas in each one relate to or allow you to comment on another?

● Queen bee
● An old queen
● The Red Queen

Focus on: inset tales

READ AND LINK . . .
— Miss Mead tells the story of Cupid and Psyche on pp. 41–3. Look up the story in a dictionary of classical mythology, or read it in a collection of myths of Greece and Rome. Robert Graves's retelling of the stories is a useful place to start. Consider the ways in which Miss Mead's version of the story diverges from the conventional tellings of the story. Then compare the ways in which this story may set out themes or issues that go with the events that are unfolding in the novella as a whole. In the course of the story you will encounter several different kinds of narrative. Keep a list of these different forms and

consider the ways that *how* you tell a story is as important as *what kind* of story you tell.

Focus on: sorting, tasks and trials

LOOK FOR A PATTERN . . .

— On pp. 41–4, Miss Matty and William hold a conversation about sorting, and the ways in which cataloguing or sorting is often used as a task demanded of fairy-tale heroes and heroines. Consider this as a proposition. What kinds of tests can you think of in fairy tales that work in this way? Jot down as many as you can. Remember that William too is currently engaged on a project that requires him to sort and catalogue, and put things in order. How does this idea relate to the themes of the story overall? What other kind of trial are the heroes and heroines of fairy stories required to complete? Think about the story of Rumpelstiltskin, or the story of the seven wild swans. What kinds of elements do these contain? Here is a list to help you:

- Suffering
- Patience
- Minute attention to detail
- Metamorphosis
- Silence
- Self-abnegation

SECTION 6
(pp. 44–55)

Focus on: Eugenia

CHARACTERISE . . .

— How would you describe Eugenia, given the (comparatively)

little that we – and William – know about her? So far, what do you think her chief characteristics and motives to be?

Focus on: colour

INTERPRET . . .
— In the interview (pp. 14–16), Byatt speaks about the ways in which she likes to 'colour-code' her novels. If you have read her novel *Possession*, you will know that green and white especially, but light and dark also, are important there. In this section of 'Morpho Eugenia', there are several allusions to colour: mainly white, grey, black, yellow, lavender. How do images of colour connect to themes in the story overall?

Focus on: male and female

ANALYSE . . .
— Differences between male and female has been a running theme from the opening of the story. How does this episode contribute to that topic?

Focus on: metamorphosis

ASSESS . . .
— Transfiguration, metamorphosis, change, alteration . . . all of these have been referred to in the course of the story so far. Who or what is transfigured in this section? How much of those changes are real – that is, to do with the facts of experience – and how much is to do with the transfiguring power of the imagination? In particular, is Eugenia changed, or is she the same?

SECTION 7
(pp. 56–63)

Focus on: natural selection

MAKE CONNECTIONS . . .

— "'You have courage, and intelligence, and kindness,'" said Eugenia's father. "'All families stand in need of these qualities if they are to survive'" (p. 56). Eugenia's father speaks to William about his proposal to marry his daughter. If you have been making notes on Darwin's theories of natural selection, use this quotation to assess the ways in which this remark may connect to the themes of the story.

Focus on: allusions

INVESTIGATE . . .

— Focus on this section and make a list of all the various literary and historical references that you can find. These will include: Alfred Tennyson's poems, William Paley, Charles Darwin, John Bunyan's *The Pilgrim's Progress*. Research any one of these and see how your new information can help to enlighten your reading of this section.

Focus on: men and women and breeding

ANALYSE . . .

— William, Edgar and Robin have a discussion about marriage – and other things – on pp. 60–3. What do you make of these exchanges? Why do you suppose that Edgar is so aggressive?

RESEARCH AND ASK YOURSELF . . .

— What are 'eugenics'? If you do not know, look the word up in a dictionary. How might that term relate to this story? Consider the significance of Eugenia's name.

SECTION 8
(pp. 63–9)

Focus on: breeding

RELATE . . .
— How many images, used in this section to depict William and Eugenia's relationship, have you already encountered in the passages of the short story more obviously related to the natural world, and to the Darwinian theories under discussion here?

SECTION 9
(pp. 69–72)

Focus on: fairy tales

EVALUATE . . .
— 'And so he lived happily ever after?' (p. 69). How far does William's story mimic or undercut the traditional terms of the fairy tale?

Focus on: proverbs

THINK ABOUT . . .
— Consider proverbs about fathers and children. Find as many as you can. And then look at pp. 70–2 where William and Eugenia's first children are born. Consider the proverb 'It takes a wise child to know its own father'. What about fathers knowing their own children? What do you think is going on here?

SECTION 10
(pp. 72–82)

Focus on: the individual and the group

ANALYSE . . .
— William is unhappy (p. 72). Why is this? In what ways is he connected to the group, species, community in which he lives? In what ways is he separate from them? Why is this significant in terms of the themes and overall concerns of the short story?

Focus on: allusions

LOOK UP . . .
— Miss Mead and Miss Matty refer to Robert Browning's poems 'Home Thoughts from Abroad' and to Milton's description of Pandemonium in *Paradise Lost* (pp. 78–80). Miss Mead then alludes to Harriet Beecher Stowe's propagandist parable *Uncle Tom's Cabin* (p. 80). Look up any or all of these works.
— Then consider how many of the following they have in common:

- Home
- Expulsion
- Family connections
- Improper connections
- Exile
- Loss
- Paradise
- Nostalgia
- Power
- Exploitation
- Inappropriate breeding
- Consanguinity

— Bearing this list in mind, ask yourself what the significance of the allusions may be.

SECTION 11
(pp. 82–90)

Focus on: nature

ACCOUNT FOR . . .
— On p. 82, the winter activities of Eugenia's brothers are described. Account for what they are doing, first of all in relation to their own characters as you understand them so far, and then as you understand them metaphorically. Remember that this is a story about 'nature' and about theories on the organisation of the natural world.

Focus on: the Bible and Darwin and poetry

READ AND NOTE . . .
— Harald Alabaster's disquisition, as given in extract here, begins with a quotation from Psalm 139. Look up this psalm in the Old Testament. Then look over all of the psalms – several of which are generally supposed to have been written by King David – and note down those that are about the natural world and which set up an attitude of praise for the glories of the natural world. Consider how this biblical background might be influencing Harald's arguments.

READ AND COMPARE . . .
— Read some of Charles Darwin's work on 'natural selection' from *On the Origin of Species*, such as in the Norton edition edited by Philip Appleman. Then compare the attitude of wonder and praise that characterises the biblical text with the

more analytical and questioning perspective that marks out Darwin's views. Which 'side' is Harald on? Which 'side' is William on?

RESEARCH . . .
— In the early twenty-first century there is still a great deal of resistance in some quarters to Darwin's theories of evolution. In the United States in particular some schools and colleges would prefer to adopt a 'creationist' explanation for the world – that is, one based on the account of God creating the world in six days as found in the Book of Genesis in the Bible. Look out some contemporary debates on this issue by using the Internet to research 'creationist' philosophy. What is it about Darwin's theories that is so unpalatable to creationists?

INFER . . .
— On pp. 87–8, Harald's treatise is supposed to include lengthy quotations from Tennyson's important and influential poem *In Memoriam* (1850). This poem was written over a number of years in response to the early death in 1833 of Arthur Hallam, Tennyson's close friend and mentor from his days studying at Cambridge. *In Memoriam* is a meditation on loss and on the contradiction of nature's way in allowing the extinction of the individual while the community or race continues. It is also a reverie on God's relation to man and the possibilities of an afterlife. Read the quoted sections carefully and list the ideas that are set out there. What does it suggest about the character of Harald's argument that the two sources that he cites in opposition to Darwin's theories – the psalms and *In Memoriam* – are both poetic texts?

Focus on: Queens

LOOK BACK AND RELATE . . .
— Part of Harald's argument relies on his understanding of the function of the queen bee in the hive (pp. 85–6). Look back at the work you have already done on 'Queens' (Section 5) and compare it with the information you are given in this section.

SECTION 12
(pp. 90–4)

Focus on: cryptic clues

CONSIDER THE CLAIM . . .
— Miss Matty assists in the presentation of a charade where the answer is 'Amazon' (pp. 91–2). In what ways might you read the whole of this story as a 'parable' or a set of 'clues' like that in a crossword puzzle? What clues are you given as to what might be going on? Remember the parallels concerning breeding and natural selection, the comparisons with the hive and the formicary, the butterflies and their processes of metamorphosis. Jot down as many of these metaphoric interconnections as you can think of and consider the claim that the story itself may be a 'puzzle' for you – the reader – to interpret.

SECTION 13
(pp. 94–105)

Focus on: more clues and parables

EVALUATE . . .
— Miss Matty has proposed the setting up of an 'ant watch'

with a view to writing up their observations as a playful kind of natural history (p. 93). Now the project begins. Consider the ways in which Matty and William's enterprise might be compared with our own enterprise as readers 'observing' the community at 'Bredely Hall'. Remember to add in the fact of that name to your calculations.

Focus on: analogy

ANALYSE . . .

— On p. 100 William says, 'Analogy is a slippery tool . . . Men are not ants.' Look up the term 'analogy' in the glossary. Then ask yourself whether or not you agree with William's remark. In what ways is the very method of this story inviting us to use 'analogy' throughout as a means of understanding and interpreting what we read?

Focus on: narrative and genre

DISTINGUISH . . .

— Read the sections on pp. 97–9 and 100–3 which purport to be extracts from William's account of the ant watch and where he describes the 'slaving raid' and the 'wedding dance'. How would you label the kind of narrative genre that William is adopting? Consider the kinds of language he uses; consider the way he builds pace and tension into his story; consider the feelings or emotional reactions that he is trying to foster in the responses of his readers. Here is a list to help you in selecting your definitions:

- Romance
- War story
- Adventure
- Comedy

- Satire
- Slapstick
- Quest
- History
- Parody
- Biography
- Farce

COMPARE . . .
— Now look at the sonnet by John Clare that Matty quotes on p. 104. How does this compare as a narrative with the stories that William has told?

Focus on: characterisation

ASSESS AND COMPARE . . .
— William thinks about Matty (p. 105). What do you make of his attitudes towards her? What do you think of her yourself? How does she compare with a) Eugenia, and b) Amy, the little 'beetle sprite'? Finally ask yourself this: if each of these three women were to be compared to an insect, what kind of insect would they be? Think of colouring, shape, behaviour, occupation.

SECTION 14
(pp. 105–8)

Focus on: nature and nurture

INTERPRET . . .
— Robin and William hold a conversation about Robin's childless state and William's many offspring (p. 106). 'It is as though environment were everything and inheritance

127

nothing,' William says. Think about this conversation and William's reverie. What do you think is going on?

Focus on: centaur or satyr

RESEARCH . . .

— Find out about 'centaurs' and 'satyrs' in classical mythology. Discover who they were, what they were and what kinds of things they did. Edgar is described as being of this 'nature' (p. 106). Then consider how this helps you assess Edgar's character; and how this comparison may relate to other half-animal / half-human beings that we have encountered elsewhere in the story so far.

SECTION 15
(pp. 108–41)

Focus on: storytelling

TRACE . . .

— Look back at Section 13 on pp. 94–105 and think again about the exercise on genre there. Then consider these additional excerpts from William and Matty's book and work out the genre and the kinds of story they are telling.

Focus on: the theme of sorting and naming

LINK . . .

— William and Matty's book includes a title page which explains the character of their project. Note that the title of the second chapter is 'The Naming and Mapping of the Colonies'. How does this section relate to the theme of sorting and naming in the story overall? How many other examples of cataloguing and ordering and sorting can you find in the story?

Focus on: 'instinct and intelligence'

ANALYSE AND ILLUSTRATE . . .

— William's story focuses on 'instinct' versus 'intelligence' as he applies these terms to his observations of the ant colony. Read over this section and sort out his various arguments. Then think back over the story as a whole and ask yourself who acts according to 'instinct' and who acts according to 'intelligence'. Which was William governed by when he desired and married Eugenia? Which governed his actions when he set out to study the ant colony? Which is more important in the characterisation of Eugenia? Or Edgar? Or Lady Alabaster? Or Matty?

Focus on: parables and parallels

COMPARE AND CRITICALLY EVALUATE . . .

— Matty responds to William's draft of the ant colony observations with a fairy story of her own, 'Things Are Not What They Seem' (pp. 119–40). Read her story and work out the ways in which both William, in his way, and Matty, in hers, are dealing with the same kinds of topics and philosophical concerns.

Focus on: fairy tales

DISCERN NARRATIVE CHARACTERISTICS . . .

— How do you know that Matty's story is a fairy tale? You might list the fact that it begins with the words 'There was once . . .', or that the farmer in the story has *three* sons. See how many other elements you can find that are related to the genre and character of fairy tale.

EXPLAIN THE NAMING . . .

— Miss Cottitoe Pan Demos explains the meaning of her name (p. 122). Look over all the names in this story and see how often you can work out some significance in the names of the characters. Then relate your conclusions to the work you have already done on the names of the characters in the story overall. There are sections about naming on pp. 131–2 and 134–5.

Focus on: myths and legends

RESEARCH . . .

— Matty's story makes reference to several classical myths and legends including Proserpina, Circe, Morpheus. Jot down as many of these as you can find and look up their stories in a dictionary of classical mythology. How do they relate to or underline the story that Matty tells?

Focus on: allegory

ASSESS . . .

— William reads Matty's story as an allegory about the Church and attitudes to the natural world (p. 141). Though Matty denies the seriousness of her 'message', how is allegory an important method in this story overall? If you are unfamiliar with the term, look it up in the glossary.

SECTION 16
(pp. 142–7)

Focus on: genre

CRITICALLY EVALUATE . . .

— On p. 144 is the text of the letter of acceptance that William and Matty receive from the publisher. Evaluate the terms that he uses to describe their work and assess how far they accord with your own view of what you have read.

Focus on: William, Edgar, Amy

CONSIDER . . .
— Weigh up the different degrees of responsibility here. What do you think of Edgar's behaviour and attitudes? Given what William had witnessed in the scullery, what do you think of his behaviour and attitudes? William asks himself the same question (on p. 147) in relation to his own experiences in the jungle.

SECTION 17
(pp. 147–53)

Focus on: plotting

ASK YOURSELF . . .
— Who do you think has sent for William?

Focus on: cryptic clues

INTERPRET . . .
— Lady Alabaster, Matty, Miss Mead, the children and William play Anagrams. Consider how this episode works and what it reveals about the characters involved and about the story overall. Then comment on the functions of clues, hints and deceptions in the story as a whole.

SECTION 18
(pp. 154–60)

Focus on: naming and allusion

CONSIDER . . .

— Why do you suppose that Matty now wants to be known as Matilda?

RESEARCH . . .

— Find out about a famous historical couple called 'William and Matilda'. Then look back at Section 4 (pp. 21–36) and the exercise on naming. How do William's and Matilda's names contrast with the names of the Alabasters? If you look at the interview (p. 23), you will see that Byatt comments on this.

Focus on: natural and unnatural

RELATE TO THE WHOLE . . .

— Eugenia says that what she did felt 'natural' (p. 159). William says it was out of nature. How does this discussion relate to the themes of the story as a whole?

Focus on: endings and beginnings

RESEARCH AND LINK . . .

— Find out about the story of Calypso in Greek legend. Why might William and Matty's ship be given this name? Why might it be appropriate that this story should end on a ship? Arturo Papagay says, 'That is the main thing . . . To be alive' (p. 160). Consider the ways in which this statement is both an end and a beginning.

Looking over the whole story

QUESTIONS FOR DISCUSSION OR ESSAYS

1. 'Nature was smiling and cruel, that was clear' (p. 32). In what ways is this remark illustrated with the scenes and actions depicted in 'Morpho Eugenia'?

2. 'Transfiguration is not a bad thing. Butterflies come out of the most unpromising crawling things' (p. 49). Consider the ways in which this remark might apply to the events depicted in this short story.

3. 'Let us, like Him, speak in parables' (p. 84). How are 'parables' of all kinds employed in 'Morpho Eugenia'?

4. 'Things Are Not What They Seem'. Why might this be an appropriate subtitle for this story?

5. List and analyse the kinds of narrative method used in this story.

6. Discuss the opposition set up in this story between William and Matilda and the Alabasters.

7. Consider the ways in which the image of the butterfly is used in this story.

8. How does the overall title of these two stories – *Angels & Insects* – connect to the themes and images set out in 'Morpho Eugenia'?

'THE CONJUGIAL ANGEL'

Focus on: the title

LOOK UP . . .
— Find the word 'conjugial' in a dictionary. Then look up 'conjugal'. Which is the word more commonly used? What is implied by the use of the more unusual word?

CHAPTER I
(pp. 163–71)

Focus on: beginnings

CONSIDER . . .
— In what ways are you drawn into this story? What is Lilias Papagay's 'profession'? Where have you heard her name before?

Focus on: poetry

RELATE . . .
— '. . . of imagination all compact' (p. 163) is a quotation from a speech about poetry and the role of the imagination that you will find in Shakespeare's *A Midsummer Night's Dream* (1595–6), Act V, scene 1. The speech begins, 'The lunatic, the lover, and the poet / Are of imagination all compact . . .' As you read on through this short story, consider how these three types of persons might each be connected to the idea of 'imagination'. And also consider how 'lunatics', 'lovers' and 'poets' figure in this story overall.

Focus on: insects and angels

NOTE THE ALLUSIONS . . .

— While this is an entirely new story – set in 1875, whereas 'Morpho Eugenia' was set in the 1860s – there are connections between the two novellas. Look out for as many as you can. For instance, on p. 163 Lilias's costume is described as being like that of a 'dragonfly'. And then – on p. 164 – Lilias draws Sophy's attention to the image of an 'angel' in the sunset. Keep a note of all such references and allusions so that you can build up connections between the two stories.

Focus on: setting

DESCRIBE AND DEFINE . . .

— The narrative tells us a lot of detail about Mrs Jesse's drawing room. Read the passage through, then close the book and write down as many details as you can remember. What is the atmosphere of this room like? How crowded with furniture and things is it? Why is it significant that each thing, object, item is associated with something or someone else? How far is the narrative setting up a distinctly material world – as opposed to the spiritual world that all these people are there to invoke?

Focus on: coffee and tea

CONSIDER AND REMEMBER . . .

— Look at the account of the conversation about coffee and tea (pp. 166–7). Consider the implications of this conversation and remember it for later on.

Focus on: allusions and history

LOOK UP . . .

— Find out about some of the historical figures mentioned in this section. These might include Emanuel Swedenborg, the Emperor Napoleon III and Walter Scott. How does information about these characters help you to find your way through the story and its historical setting?

Focus on: connections

ASK YOURSELF . . .

— Ten years ago Arturo Papagay's ship the *Calypso* was lost (p. 168). What might this tell you about the ending of the last story in this pair of novellas? What do you already know about Arturo that might be relevant to the ways in which his (supposed) widow remembers him?

Focus on: storytelling

LINK . . .

— Captain Jesse is said to be 'like the prince in some fairy story or other' (p. 166). Where have you heard this before?

COMPARE . . .

— 'Mrs Papagay liked stories' (p. 168). How does this fact help you to assess Lilias's character? If you know Shakespeare's play *Othello* (c. 1604), ask yourself how and why Lilias might be compared with Desdemona.

CHAPTER II
(pp. 172–7)

Focus on: social class

ASSESS . . .

— The narrative tells us that the Jesses and Lilias Papagay would not have met socially but that the spiritualist connection was what brought them together. Why do you think that might be? In this chapter you will find out more about the Jesses and that will help your assessment.

Focus on: history and storytelling

GUESS THE ALLUSION . . .

— 'Mrs Jesse was the heroine of a tragic story' (p. 173). This is, in fact, one of the most famous of tragic stories in English literature. With just the information given to you on this page, can you guess who Mrs Jesse is? Or who Mrs Jesse's brother is? If not, don't worry – enough information will be given to you over the page.

CONSIDER . . .

— On pp. 174–5 we are told about a letter that Mrs Papagay was shown that had been written about Mrs Jesse by the poet Elizabeth Barrett who was later to marry Robert Browning (in 1846). In what ways is Elizabeth Barrett Browning best known to history? Does 'The Barretts of Wimpole Street' mean anything to you? If it does, then use this example to think about the ways in which history and conventional memories of history do not necessarily present the varied truths of a person's individual life.

Focus on: poetry

COMPARE . . .

On p. 175, it is explained that Mrs Jesse was the sister of Alfred Tennyson and the one who was engaged to Arthur Hallam when he died – the man for whom Tennyson wrote his famous poem of mourning *In Memoriam* (1850). A section from the poem is quoted on p. 176. As the story explains, this poem was a favourite with Queen Victoria after the death of her consort Prince Albert, as it was with many other Victorian mourners.

137

On p. 175 we are told that Mrs Papagay's own favourite Tennyson poem is *Enoch Arden* which tells the story of a man, lost at sea and presumed dead, who eventually returns home to find that his wife has long since married another man and is settled and happy. Another version of that same story is told in Elizabeth Gaskell's novel *Sylvia's Lovers* (1863).

— Research and think about any or all of these references and consider the ways in which the dead, and memories of loss or death, might haunt the living.

CHAPTER III
(pp. 177–87)

Focus on: romance

LIST AND ANALYSE . . .

— Read the passages on pp. 177–9 about Emily and her imagination and her childhood. Consider how the terms of the romance are being used here. Consider how often a 'romance' – whether of the original chivalric medieval kind, or of the Mills and Boon school – might include:

- An isolated forest
- A knight or a gentleman who may be a stranger
- A fair maiden or girl
- Magic
- Transformation
- Honour
- Secret words of love

— Then consider some or all of these titles and work out which constituents of the romance, or versions thereof, are included in each:

- Daphne du Maurier's *Rebecca*
- Anya Seton's *Katherine*
- Emily Brontë's *Wuthering Heights*
- Dante's *Inferno*
- Shakespeare's *As You Like It*

Focus on: seeing and not seeing

CONSIDER . . .

— Captain Jesse tells the well-known story of how the natives of New Zealand encountered by Captain Cook and his followers seemed to fail to see the ship anchored in the harbour, because it was so far beyond their experience and comprehension. Consider the question of seeing and not seeing. Why do you suppose that sometimes people cannot 'see' what is under their noses? How does this theme relate to the setting and the themes and concerns of the story overall?

Focus on: storytelling

CONNECT . . .

— Arthur Hallam – we are told – also loved storytelling (p. 186). In what ways does this piece of information connect to the themes of the story overall?

CONTRAST . . .

This is an extract from one of (the real) Arthur Hallam's poems called 'To the Loved One'. It was not published in his lifetime but appeared in a book edited by his father Henry Hallam called *Remains in Verse and Prose of Arthur Henry Hallam* (1834).

> My heart is happy now, beloved,
>   Albeit thy form is far away;
> A joy that will not be removed
>   Broods on me like a summer's day.

Whatever evil fate may do,
 It cannot change what has been thine;
It cannot cast those words anew,
 The gentle words I think divine.

[. . .]
Sometimes I dream thee leaning o'er
 The harp I used to love so well;
Again I tremble and adore
 The soul of its delicious swell;
Again the very air is dim
 With eddies of harmonious might,
And all my brain and senses swim
 In a keen madness of delight.

Sometimes thy pensive form is seen
 On the dear seat beside the fire;
There plainest thou with Madeline
 Or Isabella's lone desire.
He knows thee not, who does not know
 The tender flashing of thine eye
At some melodious tale of woe,
 And the sweet smile and sweeter sigh.

How oft in silent moonlight air,
 When the wide earth is full of rest,
And all things outward seem more fair
 For the inward spirit less opprest,
I look for thee, I think thee near,
 Thy tones are thrilling through my soul,
Thy dark eyes close to mine appear,
 And I am blest beyond control!

— It may be that this was a poem written to or for the young Emily Tennyson who was to become Mrs Jesse later on. In what ways does this picture of the (real) Arthur contrast with that created by Byatt?

CHAPTER IV
(pp. 187–201)

Focus on: angels and insects

COMPILE AND ASSESS . . .
— Look over this chapter and note down all the references you can find both to angels and to insects. What kinds of images and metaphors are being built up here?

Focus on: cryptic clues

LINK . . .
— The pencil performs some automatic writing (p. 197) which seems not to make sense. But in what ways does it or might it make sense? Brainstorm the images and words. Amy: where does that name come from? What does it mean? What is its Latin root? How is it related to the name 'Emily'? Use the website http://www.behindthename.com to help you. How is 'Ring a Roses' a relevant image here? Make as many connections as you can.

ANALYSE . . .
— When you have made a note of all of these things, think back to the first story here, 'Morpho Eugenia'. In what ways are you being asked – through both stories – to make metaphoric and playful connections between images not necessarily strictly related?

CHAPTER V
(pp. 201–7)

Focus on: colour

INTERPRET . . .

— In the interview (pp. 14–16), Byatt says that she often will colour-code her novels. Look over this chapter and consider how that might work here. What are the key colours and what might they represent? When you have made up your mind, keep a note of your findings, as you may want to come back to them later on.

Focus on: cryptic clues

DISTINGUISH . . .

— Sophy's automatic writing begins (pp. 203–5). Look at the scraps that she writes and at the interpretations that the participants attribute to them. Then think about what they mean to you – with or without the information you are given here. How are these fragments being used to tell a story, albeit a disconnected story, subject to invention and interpretation?

CHAPTER VI
(pp. 208–15)

Focus on: birds

LIST AND RELATE . . .

— How many references to birds can you find in this chapter? And overall throughout the story? Include both images and imaginations of birds, as well as the real feathered creatures. Remember that Mrs Jesse herself is described as a 'bird' (p. 172) and that she has a pet raven called Aaron who figures as one of the illustrations. (You might also look up the reference that explains Aaron's name in Shakepeare's play *Titus Andronicus* (c. 1592).) How might the 'birds' of this story connect to the 'Angels' and the 'Insects' of the overall title of the collection?

CHAPTER VII
(pp. 215–28)

Focus on: 'remains'

PLAY WITH WORDS . . .
— Play with the idea of 'remains'. Think of as many phrases as you can to do with this idea: all that remains; the remains of the beloved; precious remains. Remember that the book that Henry Hallam edited containing Arthur's writings was published posthumously and called *Remains in Verse and Prose of Arthur Henry Hallam*. Look at what happened to Emily Jesse's copy of that book (pp. 218–20). In what sense might she have been justified in selling what 'remained'? Alfred's poem thinks differently about 'remains' as it imagines Arthur's corpse in the churchyard (p. 221). In what sense is Emily herself expected to be a 'remain' – a memorial to Arthur (p. 218)? Are her memories, spelt out here, a kind of 'remains'?

Focus on: men and women and romance

CONSIDER AND ASSESS . . .
— The story of Emily and Arthur's love is told in terms of a strictly conventional romance. There are many elements and words and phrases here that suggest those constituents. But now look at the end of this chapter on p. 228 where Emily remembers being dissatisfied with Arthur's answers to some of her questions about the differences between men and women

143

and their special qualities. How romantic is this? With whom is Arthur's really intense intellectual relation here? What does that suggest about the realities of Emily's romance?

CHAPTER VIII
(pp. 228–42)

Focus on: life and death

CONNECT . . .

— In what ways does this story of Emily's coming back to life after the death of Arthur Hallam connect to the themes of the story that concern contacting the dead, or raising the dead? Why is Emily Jesse 'old and tough and shabby' (p. 229)? In what ways does she choose life while Alfred chooses death?

CHAPTER IX
(pp. 243–53)

Focus on: poetry and imagination

READ AND COMPARE . . .

— Sophy Sheekhy recalls several famous English poems in this chapter including Tennyson's 'Mariana' (p. 248), Keats's 'The Eve of St Agnes' (pp. 248–9) and 'Ode to a Nightingale' (pp. 251–2). Read any one or all of these poems and consider how they may also be about the visionary power of the imagination. In what ways does the poet's craft compare with Sophy's skills as a medium?

CHAPTER X
(pp. 254–74)

Focus on: poetry and the imagination

COMPARE . . .

— The scene seems to move to a room where the elderly Alfred Tennyson is attempting to prepare for bed and remembering his youth and his love for Arthur Hallam. By the end of this chapter we will realise that this is, in fact, a product of Sophy's own visionary capacity. But consider this: how far is the project that Byatt has set herself in writing this story, in itself, a kind of visionary attempt – one designed to recreate, through the 'remains' of history, an imaginary but concrete image of one whom we know to be dead, and yet whose memory haunts us still? Arthur Hallam haunted Tennyson and, through his poetry, Tennyson haunts us. Work out as many parallels as you can between the creative role of the visionary, the poet and the novelist. In particular, if you read carefully the passages included here which come from Tennyson's *In Memoriam* (1850), you will see that this resurrection of the dead is exactly the ambition of his poetic enterprise.

CHAPTER XI
(pp. 275–87)

Focus on: resurrections

RESEARCH THE COMPARISON . . .

— On p. 275 some persons are mentioned who – in history or in legend – attempted to communicate with the dead. Look up the stories of Saul and the Witch of Endor, or Odysseus and Tiresias. In what ways can you compare their stories with that being played out here?

Focus on: birds and angels

KEEP ADDING . . .

— There are yet more references to bird and angels in this chapter. Keep adding to your list and making connections to the overall picture of the image.

Focus on: clues and fragments

PURSUE . . .

— The automatic writing again produces a range of references and allusions. Look up some or all of these: Tennyson's 'Mariana', Shakespeare's *Measure for Measure*, and several allusions to phrases from the Bible. How do any of these relate to the themes of the story overall?

Focus on: marriage and the 'conjugial angel'

EVALUATE . . .

— The spirit conjured up seems to be telling Emily Jesse that she will be united in death with the long-dead Arthur Hallam. She decides that is not right, given her living husband's presence and loyalty over the years. What do you think of this conclusion?

Focus on: clues and fragments again

ANALYSE . . .

— The automatic writing spirit starts on an obscene poem. When did you realise it was going this way? What does this suggest? Why does it take this particular poetic form? (Look back over the poems cited in the story for a clue.) How does this poem undercut the high-flown sentiments of the 'spirit' world? Why is it appropriate that it's Mrs Papagay who is now the instrument?

CHAPTER XII
(pp. 288–90)

Focus on: beginnings and endings

RELATE . . .
— Connect this 'ending' of Lilias's story to the 'ending' of Emily and Richard's story in the last chapter. In each case consider whether these conclusions are based on 'spiritual' or 'material' values. Or are they balanced in between, and if so, in what way?

Looking over the whole story

QUESTIONS FOR DISCUSSION OR ESSAYS
1. Compare and contrast the characters of Emily Jesse and Lilias Papagay.

2. Consider the portrayal of the differing values that belonged to Victorian men and women as they are set out in this story.

3. Analyse the proposition that the poet and the medium are engaged on the same enterprise – the recovery of the lost voice of the dead.

4. 'The message of "The Conjugial Angel" is that the material is always valued over the spiritual.' Do you agree?

5. In the light of the events and themes in this story, consider whether ghosts are always 'accusing, unappeased' (p. 242).

Looking over the whole of Angels & Insects

QUESTIONS FOR DISCUSSION OR ESSAYS

1. Describe the ways in which these two stories are linked.

2. Compare EITHER William Adamson and Richard Jesse, OR Matilda Crompton and Emily Jesse.

3. In what ways is Arturo Papagay the appropriate link between the two stories?

4. Analyse the treatment of the theme of storytelling in both 'Morpho Eugenia' and 'The Conjugial Angel'.

5. Describe and account for the specific mixture of many different kinds of narrative form in both stories.

6. Consider the imagery of ONE of the following in both stories: angels, insects, birds, the jungle, cataloguing, visions.

Contexts, comparisons and complementary readings

These sections suggest contextual and comparative ways of reading the three texts by Byatt. You can put your reading in a social, historical or literary context. You can make comparisons – again, social, literary or historical – with other texts or art works. Or you can choose complementary works (of whatever kind) – that is, art works, literary works, social reportage or facts which in some way illuminate the text by sidelights or interventions which you can make into a telling framework. Some of the suggested contexts are directly connected to the book, in that they will give you precise literary or social frames in which to situate the novel. In turn, these are either related to the period within which the novel is set, or to the time – now – when you are reading it. Some of these examples are designed to suggest books or other texts that may make useful sources for comparison (or for complementary purposes) when you are reading *Possession, Angels & Insects* and *A Whistling Woman*. Again, they may be related to literary or critical themes, or they may be relevant to social and cultural themes current 'then' or 'now'.

Focus on: pictures

CONSIDER AND ASSESS . . .
— All the way through both of these stories there are illustrations of insects, angels, dogs and birds. Look at each of these carefully as you come across them and consider how they relate to each of their stories, and to the collection as a whole.

'MORPHO EUGENIA'

Focus on: Darwinian theory and the Victorian novel

RESEARCH AND COMPARE . . .
— The publication of Charles Darwin's *On the Origin of Species* (1859) was highly influential, and many contemporary thinkers – including the novelists – wrestled with his ideas in their works. Key texts of this kind might include: Thomas Hardy's *A Pair of Blue Eyes* (1873) and George Meredith's *The Egoist* (1879), both of which include some consideration of 'sexual selection'; and Hardy's *Jude the Obscure* (1896), which might be read as a meditation on 'the survival of the fittest'. Compare the handling of Darwinian theory in any one of these novels with Byatt's treatment of it in 'Morpho Eugenia'.

An important book on this subject is Gillian Beer's *Darwin's Plots: Evolutionary Narrative in Darwin, George Eliot and Nineteenth Century Fiction* (1982).

Focus on: narrative methods

LIST AND ANALYSE . . .

— In both 'Morpho Eugenia' and in *Possession*, and indeed in 'The Conjugial Angel', Byatt uses a mixed narrative method. Look over any one or more of these works and see how many different kinds of narrative you can find. Include various kinds of poetry, letters, journals, political argument, confessions, and any others you can think of.

— Once you have your list, ask yourself why Byatt does this. What does this achieve in the connection between the reader and the text? What does it mean about the different kinds of 'voices' that Byatt can produce as a result?

RESEARCH AND COMPARE . . .

— As Byatt is a professional *reader* as well as a writer – in that she worked for some years as an eminent university teacher – she thinks, in her fiction too, about the methods of reading and the methods of storytelling. Read her collection of selected essays called *On Histories and Stories* (2001) to see the ways in which she thinks about her own crafts of writing and reading.

'THE CONJUGIAL ANGEL'

Focus on: imagination

READ AND RELATE . . .

The first line of this story is 'Lilias Papagay was of imagination all compact' (p. 163). This is a quotation from *A Midsummer Night's Dream*. Here is the text of the whole speech:

The lunatic, the lover, and the poet
Are of imagination all compact:
One sees more devils than vast hell can hold;
That is the madman; the lover, all as frantic,
Sees Helen's beauty in a brow of Egypt:
The poet's eye, in a fine frenzy rolling,
Doth glance from heaven to earth, from earth to heaven,
And, as imagination bodies forth
The forms of things unknown, the poet's pen
Turns them to shapes, and gives to airy nothing
A local habitation and a name.
Such tricks hath strong imagination,
That, if it would but apprehend some joy,
It comprehends some bringer of that joy;
Or in the night, imagining some fear,
How easy is a bush supposed a bear?

Act V, scene 1

— Read over this speech and consider the ways in which its terms may also relate to Byatt's story 'The Conjugial Angel'.
— When you have done that, think also about the play as a whole. In what ways might you be able to make a comparison between Shakespeare's play and Byatt's short story? Consider the fairy visitations to the human world; consider the transformation of Bottom; consider also the mix-up between the lovers and relate each of these elements to some similar situation in Byatt's story.

RESEARCH . . .
— Look up the word 'imagination' in a dictionary of quotations. How many quotations do you find and from what kinds of sources? How often is it poets who write about the power of the imagination? In Byatt's story who experiences the most intense imagined scenes – a poet, a lover, someone mad with loss?

Focus on: spiritualist phenomena

RESEARCH . . .

— Look up some modern examples of the spiritualist. In 1931, the spiritualist Noah Zerdin founded the Link of Home Circles. You can find out about his work and the Noah's Ark Society by looking up the website www.noahsarksoc.fsnet.co.uk/about nas.htm and you can read an interview with Noah Zerdin at www.leslieflint.com/interview.html. There, you will find that Zerdin set up seances in London in the 1930s. Use the information you find to help you reflect on the scenes played out in 'The Conjugial Angel'.

VINTAGE
LIVING
TEXTS

A Whistling Woman

IN CLOSE-UP

Reading guides for

A WHISTLING WOMAN

BEFORE YOU BEGIN TO READ . . .
— Read the interview with Byatt. You will see there that she identifies a number of themes and techniques:

- Allusion
- Storytelling
- The natural world

Other themes that may be useful to consider while reading the novel include:

- Birds, bird-women and snails
- Victim and predator
- Blood
- The mind
- Madness and psychosis
- Learning and education
- The idea of the university

Reading activities: detailed analysis

Focus on: the title and the epigraphs

THINK ABOUT . . .

— Consider the saying connecting a 'Whistling Woman' and 'Crowing Hen'. Think about traditional views of women, what sort of 'folk wisdom' they come from, and why this is offered to us now. What do you suppose Byatt's take on the saying may be, given that she cites this quotation as 'a frequent saying of my maternal grandmother'. Byatt comments on the title in the interview (pp. 29–30).

— You will see that the inside of the cover is ornamented with an elaborate picture of various kinds of exotic birds in a landscape which includes a distant city. Write yourself some notes on this image and what it suggests to you. Look again at the picture and your own notes when you have read to the end of the novel and consider how your first reactions compare with your later feelings and opinions of the novel.

THINK ABOUT PROVERBS . . .

— Look up in a dictionary of proverbs the entries under 'woman'. How many proverbs can you find that are about women and what they should be or how they should be treated?

Examples might include:

- A woman, a dog and a walnut tree, the better you beat them, the better they be.
- A woman and a ship ever want mending.
- A woman's place is in the home.
- A woman's work is never done.

— How many others can you find? What does this suggest about conventional attitudes to women in the Western world?
— Now look up 'man' in a dictionary of proverbs. You might find examples like:

- Man cannot live by bread alone.
- Man is the measure of all things.
- Man proposes, God disposes.
- The man who is born in a stable is not a horse.
- Manners maketh man.

— What do you notice about the ways that these proverbs understand the term 'man' and the term 'woman'?
— If you had to put in order the hierarchy of these terms in relation to the norms represented by this (or any other) selection of proverbs, how would it go?

- Woman
- Ships
- God
- Dogs
- Walnut trees
- Bread
- Home
- Man
- Horses

Focus on: the epigraphs

RESEARCH AND CONSIDER . . .

— Look at the extract from *Alice in Wonderland* which reports the conversation between Alice-as-serpent and the pigeon. If you have read Lewis Carroll's books *Alice's Adventures in Wonderland* and *Through the Looking-Glass*, or have a chance to look them up, think of the ways in which Alice changes shape so frequently.

— If you have already read Byatt's *Possession*, think of the way in which Melusina changes, or metamorphoses, into a snake below the waist each Saturday, and why.

— What is the effect of such change likely to be on beings? Would you start to see things from a wider perspective? How would others see you?

— In the excerpt from Andrew Marvell's poem 'The Garden', consider the potential that Marvell invests in the bird. What might Byatt be suggesting by putting together so many references to birds and women?

CHAPTER I
(pp. 1–16)

Focus on: storytelling and beginnings and endings

INTERPRET . . .

— *A Whistling Woman* is the final part of Byatt's quartet of novels following the fortunes of Frederica Potter from youth to middle age. The other books in the series are *The Virgin in the Garden* (1978), *Still Life* (1985) and *Babel Tower* (1996). Consider the fact that Byatt has chosen to open this novel with the final pages of a children's story. What type of atmosphere does this give to the novel?

— How do you feel about Agatha (and Byatt) leaving the story of Artegall, Mark and Dracosilex at this point? Do you share Leo's wish that Agatha would continue the story? How filmable do you think Agatha's story could be?

— Beginnings and endings are both here in the first few pages. As we are introduced to Frederica Potter at the beginning of the novel, she is already considering the end of her affair with John Ottokar (pp. 12–13). How does this connect to other themes?

Focus on: birds and snails, predators and victims

EXPLORE . . .

— Where we pick up Agatha's story at the beginning of the novel, Artegall is talking to a thrush. (If you have a look at the beginning of *Babel Tower*, you will see that that novel also starts with a thrush. In that case the thrush is predatory, crushing a snail.) Birds and snails appear in both these novels. What does the image of the bird suggest to you? What key ideas would you associate with birds? Here is a list to help you:

- Claws and talons
- Flight
- Freedom
- Wings
- Haunting
- Threatening
- Pecking
- Caged
- Preying

— Then ask yourself the same question about snails. Again, here is a list to help you:

- Slimy
- Preyed on
- Housed
- Fragile
- Intricate
- Whorled
- Vulnerable

— If you had to assign roles to birds and to snails, metaphorically speaking, would you see each as victims? Or predators?

RESEARCH AND COMPARE . . .
— Read Daphne du Maurier's well-known short story called 'The Birds' which was made into an even more famous film by Alfred Hitchcock. How is the idea of the bird portrayed there? And are they presented as victims or predators? Keep all this in mind as you make links with the themes of Byatt's novel.

Focus on: the Whistlers

CONNECT . . .
— Consider how the Whistlers are described. Look at the way in which they are shown as both predators and also victims. In what ways might you be able to make connections between the Whistlers and their activities here, and the 'Whistling Woman' of the title and the epigraph to the novel?
— Notice the way in which Artegall has changed his declaration when he arrives at the city. Why might this be? What has happened along the way to change him?

Focus on: love, doubleness and comparison

ASK YOURSELF . . .
— Consider what it might be like to have a lover who was

163

one of twins. If the twins are identical, how would you feel if you could not tell them apart? How does Frederica feel for John, and for her son Leo? Do you think it likely that 'she might even die for Leo' (p. 16)? Is this statement about mother love really always the case? Might there be some exceptions to this situation? Is it exaggerated?

CHAPTER II
(pp. 17–25)

Focus on: snails

RESEARCH AND COMPARE . . .
Jacqueline Winwar's work is on the changes and evolutions of snail communities. If you have read Byatt's short story 'Morpho Eugenia' in *Angels & Insects*, you will appreciate Byatt's interest in Charles Darwin's theories of evolution as set out in his books *On the Origin of Species* (1859) and *The Descent of Man* (1870). In 'Morpho Eugenia' the interest is addressed to communities of ants; in *A Whistling Woman* the focus is snails. As this novel is set in 1968, another factor brought into consideration is the discovery of the structure of DNA. Jacqueline also refers to Konrad Lorenz. Jacqueline quotes his writings saying that 'we have "*an absolute ignorance of the physiological mechanisms underlying learning*"' (p. 21).
— How interesting, or how successful, do you think Jacqueline's work on snails would be? Consider the type of activities it would entail. Notice how the narrative speaks of Jacqueline and Luk working at 'snail-level and snail-speed' (p. 18). If you were to try and understand learning and the way minds work, how would you go about it? Why do you think that Jacqueline is working on snails at this time?

Focus on: characterisation

ASSESS . . .

— What do you notice about Lucy Nighby, and her husband Gunner who is briefly referred to? What is implied in some of the silences in Luk and Jacqueline's conversation with Lucy? What is suggested about the dynamics between Luk and Jacqueline? The narrative line raises questions about unsuccessful love — what is the relationship between these two? The chapter ends with a dream that Luk experiences. This too connects the image of woman and the image of the bird. What do you think this dream means? What does it suggest about Luk's character and the values that are important to him?

CHAPTER III
(pp. 26–35)

Focus on: the theme of naming

ASSESS . . .

— Contemplate the letters making up the acronym NYU. What do they represent for most people from all over the world? Think also about the Vice-Chancellor's name. Why do you think that it includes an allusion to 'nobel' and what does this suggest?

— Look up the Nobel Prize on the Internet. Remember that prizes are given by the Swedish foundation for peace and also for certain areas of knowledge and achievement. Who was Nobel? Why is the prize named after him?

— It is one of Byatt's novelistic traits to load the names that she chooses with symbols or sounds that may be meaningful or significant, or capable of inventive interpretation. What sort of person might 'Crowe' be, or 'Pinsky', 'Eichenbaum' or 'Hodgkiss'?

Focus on: characterisation

DECIDE . . .

— What do you think of the practical joke, the 'barbed joke' left by Wijnnobel's wife among the papers on Wijnnobel's desk (p. 30)? How would you react to it yourself?

— Think about the way in which she is brightening up the cloakroom. Ask yourself whether it is right that we should take over the properties in which we live – or, alternatively, should we try to preserve certain things for those who come after us to enjoy them?

— What are the interests of Eva Selkett–Wijnnobel? Look up the names she has given to her cat Bastet, her dogs Odin and Frigg, and the name that she gives herself, 'Selket'. Also notice her interest in Yeats, Vaughan, Jung and Hermes Trismegistus. If you don't recognise these references and their contexts, look them up. Some information on each of them will be given to you later in the text. Also ask yourself what it suggests that you – along with many others – may not early recognise these references.

Focus on: body and mind

CONSIDER AND ASSESS . . .

— In discussing the conference of Body and Mind, Gerard considers Freud, Jung, Klein, in the field of psychiatry. What do you think about the historic encounter between Hodder Pinsky and his psycho-linguistics, and Theobald Eichenbaum and his work on learning? Do you think intellectuals should be held accountable for the ideas and politics of their time, as Eichenbaum is here said to have compromised with Fascism? Apply these ideas to contemporary events. For instance, how do you think this episode might relate to the interests and anxieties of someone working in President George W. Bush's America, or Saddam Hussain's Iraq?

Focus on: art, preferences and implications

RESEARCH AND CONSIDER . . .
— Wijnnobel decorates his home with works by the – very different – artists, Rembrandt and Mondrian. Try to look at a couple of paintings of each – do a search on the Internet for each name. Then consider what might make someone enjoy and appreciate the works of two such very different artists.

Focus on: the theme of blood

IMAGINE AND INTERPRET . . .
— The chapter ends with a visit to a man in Cedar Mount – which is a kind of psychiatric institution. This man is having visions of blood. Notice his struggle with his visions, as well as his attempts to keep a hold on everyday life and to interact with others. Imagine what might lie behind such visions. Write down a list of the main themes that you think might be collecting around this image of blood – blood as a life-giving force, and blood shed as a focus for the deprivation of life and fraught with the possibility of contamination.

CONTRAST AND COMPARE . . .
— Look up the speeches by Lady Macbeth that appear in Acts I and V of Shakespeare's *Macbeth* (c. 1606). How do ideas connected with blood as they are set out there relate to the images here in the novel?

RESEARCH . . .
— Look up the key word 'blood' in a dictionary of quotations. How many other references and allusions can you find that set up similar ideas? Why are we so interested in images and associations to do with blood and the loss of blood?

CHAPTER IV
(pp. 36–51)

Focus on: tradition and experiment

WEIGH UP . . .
— Return to Frederica who is resigning because she wishes to teach. Her students, on the other hand, aren't interested in learning. They are agitating, worrying, making new connections to other areas of interest and are less focused on the subjects Frederica wishes to teach. Consider the consequences of abolishing tradition and the practices of the past. Why might we need what has gone before? Of what value is the past? In what ways does this connect to the themes of the novel as a whole?

RESEARCH . . .
— Look up the plot of D. H. Lawrence's novel *Lady Chatterley's Lover* (1928). Why might the students wish to study this book? If you've never read the book, what else do you know about it that might make it attractive as an option for a course?

Focus on: learning and teaching

ASK YOURSELF . . .
— What would you do in Frederica's situation? What types of learning methods work for you? Do you prefer a lecture, a seminar or a discussion? Would it be good to abolish classes, exams, etc.? How much would you learn if such practice were universally accepted?
— How does what Frederica says to her students relate to her own personal work, collecting cut-ups and making a 'laminated system' out of them? Do you enjoy reading her cut-ups?

Focus on: other methods of communication

CONSIDER . . .

— The rest of the chapter introduces Frederica's television work. Look out for various reactions to this work, which is seen, as it is screened, by most of the other characters of the book, throughout the novel. Each time characters react in various ways. Why does Edmund Wilkie call this project *Through the Looking-Glass*? Consider this early use of TV, and also some of the other types of programmes which have developed since then. What are your favourite types of programmes? Would you watch the type of programme which Frederica starts to introduce?

Focus on: narrative method and style

CONTRAST AND COMPARE . . .

— Look at the interview between Mickey Impey (notice the symbolism of his name) and Frederica. What sort of impression do we get of Impey from his badges/buttons? Or his poem on p. 39?

— In putting this poem into a book which is also very full of scientific discussion, Byatt is making some complex statements about discourses and narrative method. She also highlights some of the weaknesses of Impey's approach. How is he described, how does he talk to Frederica, and how successful is his interview in comparison with hers? At the same time his poem is creative in a way that Frederica's *Laminations* do not quite attempt to be. What does this suggest about the merits and weaknesses of both?

Focus on: allusion and reference

RESEARCH . . .

— Frederica and Wilkie mention Plato's Cave, Vietnam, the Falklands, T. S. Eliot. If you are not familiar with any of these references, look them up and consider how they help you to frame the historical context of the book.

Focus on: colour

ASSESS AND ASK YOURSELF . . .

— Frederica talks about the effect of colour on the TV experience. Can you imagine watching programmes in monochrome alone? How does watching black-and-white films affect your experience and enjoyment of cinema?

CHAPTER V
(pp. 52–78)

Focus on: sex, men and women, and point of view

CONTEMPLATE . . .

— Consider the sexual undercurrent in the interview between Jacqueline and Lyon Bowman. How does she manage to interest him in her research? Why does he take her on in spite of his misgivings? How good or bad are we at getting outside our own perspective, or our own sex, and seeing things from the other person's, or other sex's, point of view? How much do characters in novels help us in this type of understanding?

Focus on: clues

THINK ABOUT . . .

— Much of this chapter continues with correspondence between Kieran Quarrell, psychiatrist at Cedar Mount, and Elvet Gander, psychoanalyst, who is connected to the Spirit's Tigers. Kieran talks about a patient, Josh Lamb. Why do you think he hopes to get him out of the institution and into the Spirit's Tigers? What clues do we have as to Josh's past, his areas of interest, and what could possibly have happened to him to bring him to this institution?

Focus on: themes of light and dark

MAKE COMPARISONS . . .

— Manichaeism was founded on a radical dualism, and taught that reality consists of two great forces eternally opposed to each other, Good (that is, God, Truth, Light) and Evil, or Darkness, the latter being identified with matter. As he exists, man is tragically involved in the material order; he is fallen and lost. However, he is a particle of Light, belonging to, though exiled from, the transcendent world. He is of the same essence as God, and human souls are fragments of the divine substance. If you are interested in this area of discussion; look up J. N. D. Kelly's *Early Christian Doctrines* (1968).

— Canon Adelbert Holly and his book *Within God Without God, Our Passions Christ's Passion* is a disguised allusion to John Robinson the Bishop of Woolwich and his book *Honest to God* (1963), which is an attempt to get away from the transcendence of God and to bring Him to a closer level with humanity. If you can look this up and consider the connection.

Focus on: the theme of microcosm and macrocosm

LOOK OVER . . .

— While Marcus, Jac and Luk are working on their snails (about to be superseded by the discovery of the DNA helix by Crick, Watson and Franklin), action breaks through theory with the arrival of a bloody sheepdog. Consider how much of this 'domestic mayhem' you had guessed at from the last meeting with Lucy. Who is responsible for what happens here? What is suggested in the symbolism of the stained-glass window? Again, Byatt plays with beginnings and endings, in suggesting violence to come later. What do you think this might be? What sort of effect is such trauma likely to have on children? What is the suggestion of the narrative transition to Josh Lamb and his visions of blood? The story tells of his father instructed by an angel to smother his family to save them from the coming holocaust. What sort of logic does this offer, or what type of mindset could hold responsibility for the death of his family members in this way? What is the likely effect of the violence on Lucy's children?

CHAPTER VI
(pp. 79–89)

Focus on: parody

ANALYSE . . .

— In reading this chapter, consider why the leaflets of the Anti-University blew between the towers. What part do Marx and Mao-Tse-Tung play in this revolutionary debate?

— Look at one of the protesting lists. For instance, 'The Anti-University is coming . . .' on p. 80. How would you rate these protested items – anti-teaching, then anti-students, anti-Christ, anti-capitalism, anti-hamburgers? What is the place of anti-tealeaves, anti-overweight-currencies, and finally anti-being-anti? What do you think will be the result of bringing papers on 'The Idea of the Innate and its part in a Theory of Learning' and 'Artificial Intelligence and Cognitive Psychology. Order from Noise' to such a chaotic setting?

Focus on: wordplay

ASK YOURSELF . . .

— Byatt is a writer who is interested in wordplay and the ways in which words work. Do you think she might be having fun here? Is the reader being teased and, if so, does it matter?

CHAPTER VII
(pp. 90–110)

Focus on: symbols

RELATE . . .

— Consider the letterhead of the university as described in Elvet's letter on p.90. It is 'red and black and has rearing dragons, symbolic mound with a tree (a cedar?), and something I think is a fountain'. Then put this against the 'Anti-University' paperwork which is on 'greenish paper and is decorated with a kind of spotted-Dick effect of painted unlidded eyes – I never know if they are the Evil Eye, or an eye designed to stare down the Evil Eye, or an Evil Eye to counteract the Evil Eye' (p. 90). What are the effects of such symbols on you as a reader? What might they represent?

Focus on: memory and trauma

ASSESS . . .

— This chapter takes us into Josh Lamb's memories of his traumatic past. Why do you suppose he emphasises the boy's fat and fleshy thighs? Why does he recount his story both outside – as compassion for the boy who represents himself – and also inside the story as he remembers his own reactions?

— Try to understand 'the other' outside the window, where this being has come from, or what has created it, and what responsibilities he gives him to carry. Remember this feature for forthcoming chapters.

IMAGINE AND RECREATE . . .

— What are your feelings for the boy, for his father? Imagine the scene in the bedroom, in the coal-hole, and with the policeman. How successful was his Auntie Agnes's attempt to keep information from him? Would you do the same? Is it better to know? Or is it worse? Why does Byatt name his aunt 'Agnes'? In the text of the Requiem Mass the 'Agnus Dei' is the 'Lamb of God'. Who is this 'Lamb of God' according to the tenets of Christian iconography?

Focus on: allusion and violence

RESEARCH . . .

— Josh suffers when he reads Charles Dickens's *Oliver Twist* in school and again when someone takes him to the cinema to see the film *Kind Hearts and Coronets* (1949) (p. 99). Read two scenes from *Oliver Twist* (1837–39) – the scene showing the murder of Nancy by Bill Sikes, and the scene showing Fagin in the condemned cell. Alternatively, try to see the film – which is available on video. Then try to account for the ways in which these scenes affect Josh in the light of his experience.

Focus on: the Lamb

RESEARCH AND COMPARE . . .

— Josh's father had marked a passage in the Bible from Genesis Chapter 22, verses 6, 7, 8. The passage is on p. 100 of the novel. Read that biblical extract, think about what Josh's father had done and why. Then read this poem by Wilfred Owen and compare it with the events in the novel.

The Parable of the Old Men and the Young

So Abram rose, and clave the wood, and went,
And took the fire with him, and a knife.
And as they sojourned both of them together,
Isaac the first-born spake and said, My Father,
Behold the preparations, fire and iron,
But where the lamb for this burnt-offering?
Then Abram bound the youth with belts and straps,

And builded parapets and trenches there,
And stretchèd forth the knife to slay his son.
When lo! an angel called him out of heaven,
Saying, Lay not thy hand upon the lad,
Neither do anything to him. Behold,
A Ram, caught in a thicket by its horns;
Offer the Ram of Pride instead of him.
But the old man would not do so, but slew his son,
And half the seed of Europe, one by one.

— Owen's poem is, in part, a commentary on the sacrifice of so many young lives during the conflict of the First World War. Josh's father has committed his crime as a 'sacrifice'. The term 'holocaust' means 'a burnt offering'. How does this connect to the fact that these events take place at the beginning of the Second World War in Europe?

ASK YOURSELF . . .
— Returning to Josh Lamb's story, what is his interpretation of this extract from Genesis, and its effect on him? Look out for the type of incidents that make him black out, or lose control. Note which teachers have an influence on him. Byatt often refers to teachers – how important do you think they are or can be?

CHAPTER VIII
(pp. 111–32)

Focus on: the idea of the Church

ASSESS . . .
— Near the beginning of this chapter Lamb is trying to work out the role of the Church. Ask yourself: does it make real the

dangerous vacancies of life? Is it a fortress against them? What is a good way to deal with evil, with bad memory or trauma? Is it possible to help people recover from such dreadful experiences as that of Josh Lamb?

Focus on: revenge and forgiveness

CONSIDER . . .
— Josh personalises the Book of Joshua in the Bible (p. 114). What do you think of such Old Testament stories of revenge against enemies? How do you think they can be reconciled with a view of God as love?

Focus on: voices and 'the other self'

IMAGINE AND RELATE . . .
— Consider how Josh's voices stop as he talks to others, and also how he enjoys his reading. What do you suppose is the meaning of his babble of voices? Where are they coming from? Think of some visionaries who have been visited by voices (Joan of Arc, for example). When his voices and 'the other' return after a period of time, he calls himself the Syzygos, the Heavenly Twin. How does this naming and twinning relate to the twins John and Paul? What type of relationship does being a twin give a person? Can they operate on another plane of communication from ordinary siblings?

Focus on: memory and trauma

DECIDE . . .
— How do you feel when Josh Lamb leaves the university? Could he have achieved more, with better help and understanding for his traumas? Can such people overcome their past? Is society any better at dealing with this now?
— What do you think of the way Josh helps Lucy? Do you

think, in a way, one must become mad in order to reach the mad? What do you think of the way he offers her his Manichaean ideas, for example his ideas of light? What place is given to the physical in this encounter? Why does he dislike it so much, and why does she need it? Could this also relate to other types of appeal and revulsion between people?

CHAPTER IX
(pp. 133–47)

Focus on: television

CONSIDER . . .
— Byatt introduces Frederica's television appearances through the desire of her son Leo to watch her. How would you feel about the public appearance of someone close to you? What would be the balance of pride and embarrassment in your reaction?

INTERPRET THE CONNECTIONS . . .
— The first programme of *Through the Looking-Glass*, with Jonathan Miller and Richard Gregory, starts with Charles Dodgson – who wrote *Alice in Wonderland* (1865) under the pseudonym of Lewis Carroll – and goes on to consider Manichees, women and blood. It will be discussed from the points of view of other characters in the novel. Note that the interplay of the plot is interesting here. Leo, who has difficulty reading, can quote *Alice in Wonderland*, make very acute remarks to his mother about what they both do and should do, and also we are told, 'He knew she knew she was a parody of a mother' (p. 139). What does this mean and how might all these connections link the 'Alice' element of Frederica's television programmes with what is going on in her own life?

Focus on: mothers and sons

ASK YOURSELF . . .

— What is Frederica's relationship with motherhood? If you have read *Babel Tower*, remember her escape from her husband at the beginning, first of all without and then with Leo, in a very dramatic scene ending in a torn leg. How successfully is this mother–son relationship portrayed here? Although they argue, the arguments never become strident. Do you think Byatt is being somewhat optimistic in her portrayal of these two?

Focus on: women and feminism

MAKE CONNECTIONS AND CRITICALLY EVALUATE . . .

The second programme includes Julia Corbett and Penny Komuves. Corbett is a novelist whom Byatt writes of in an earlier novel, *The Game* (1992). She is a successful writer 'somewhere between a lady novelist and a woman novelist' (p. 140). The narrative tells us of her novel *Just a Little Bit Higher.* 'Its edge of aimlessness frightened Frederica more than the ferocity and violence of *The Golden Notebook*' (p.141).

— *The Golden Notebook* (1962), Doris Lessing's well-known classic, is an impressive and important book. If you are interested in this area, it would be a good idea to read it. In relation to this section of Byatt's novel, ask yourself some of these questions: 'What do women want?' (p. 142) Or are there as many answers as there are women? How far can the sex revolution go while women's magazines are full of hints about make-up, dress, winning one's man, etc.? How would you rate the options given in this interview – love, family, sex, certainty, naughtiness? What is the place of work and career in this schema?

RESEARCH AND CONSIDER . . .

The participants on the television show discuss George Eliot (p. 144) a nineteenth-century woman who offers us a paradox in that she lived the sexual revolution by necessity rather than choice, but also remained conservative in many ways. The books by Eliot that they discuss – *Middlemarch, Daniel Deronda, The Mill on the Floss* – generally end with their strong female characters being defeated by life and accepting a more humble role.

— Ask yourself if the twenty-first century has solved the problems of women. Can women follow their need to procreate and also create? Are we any better at juggling career and family than our grandmothers of other centuries? Will it ever be possible for women to be as free in their careers as men have always been?

ASK YOURSELF . . .
— Penny opens the possibility of parthenogenesis (p. 146). (The ancient goddess Athena sprang fully formed from the head of her father Zeus.) Perhaps sperm banks will make such a situation possible in the future. Do you think women need men? Do children need fathers?

RESEARCH . . .
— Research into the lives of Mary Wollstonecraft, Florence Nightingale and Emily Davies – all mentioned on p. 146. Are there any good examples of women successful in both public and private life? Can you make a list of men who you believe to have have been successful in both sides of their life, personal and public?

CHAPTER X
(pp. 148–61)

Focus on: sexual expression

CONSIDER . . .
— After the discussion of women's sexual needs in the previous

chapter, Frederica wonders about herself reaching a point of desiring celibacy. This may also relate to Byatt's novel *Possession*, where both Maud and Roland imagine crisp white sheets and celibacy as an escape from their private love wounds. If you have read *The Virgin in the Garden* and *Still Life*, compare Frederica now with Frederica then. Is this a significant change?

Focus on: creativity

RESEARCH AND CONSIDER . . .
— The third programme involves Hodder Pinsky and Elvet Gander and a discussion of creativity. They mention *King Lear* (c. 1605), Beethoven, Oedipus, *Hamlet* (c. 1601), *Paradise Lost* (1667). Consider what is so special, interesting or timeless about such works that it makes us come back to them.
— Pinsky's story, from Freud, from Virgil (pp. 155–6), might suggest the kinds of interdependence of ideas and connections that Byatt is trying for in all her work. She has referred to her book *Possession* as a detective story, a quest. We read to learn what happens, and we are given a personal twist at the end of the story, which we are told to relate to the characters of the novel, and not only to Frederica herself. Watch out for another reference to this classic situation later on in the novel.

ASK YOURSELF . . .
— Consider the Freud story. What do you think of Freud's juxtaposition of 'calendar, blood, origin, child-sacrifice, the avenger'? Note that the latter items in this list might be less obviously connected.

Focus on: the image of the egg

INTERPRET . . .
— Frederica mentions the Mundane Egg laid by Night (p. 158). She could also have referred to the eggs around the neck of

Artemis, goddess of childbirth, to whom Byatt indirectly refers in *Possession*, when Ash sees a hound with eggs around its neck and cannot approach LaMotte's cottage. Find some other uses of the egg in mythologies and tales of origins.

CHAPTER XI
(pp. 162–85)

Focus on: Jacqueline and Luk

WORK OUT . . .
— This chapter deals with Jacqueline's conflict between Lyon Bowman and Luk Lysgaard-Peacock. Consider Jacqueline's line of least resistance to Lyon's approach. What exactly is she objecting to in his 'good *girl*'? As you watch Luk set up a bower or love-nest, how highly do you rate their chances of success? Why does Jacqueline connect 'My lady is served' with 'good *girl*'? What role does each man assign to the woman in these words? While very different, something connects them for Jacqueline, causing their failure.

Focus on: birds

INTERPRET . . .
— Notice the bird symbolism in this chapter and consider how human and bird courtships compare in this context.

CHAPTER XII
(pp. 186–90)

Focus on: undoing and points of view

ANALYSE . . .

— Consider Luk's attitude to Frederica. Why is he so critical of her? What is it about Frederica that makes people so often react negatively towards her? Is it something that goes together with her success? Or is it possible that she receives criticism because she breaks out of more traditional gender roles?

Focus on: allusions

CONSIDER ODIN . . .

— Research Odin and find out what the relationship of this figure from Norse mythology is with Christ. Byatt has referred to this from *The Virgin in the Garden* onwards. In what ways might he be presented as a Christ alternative, and why?

CONSIDER ST PAUL . . .

— Look up the account of Paul's road to Damascus conversion in the Acts of the Apostles from the New Testament. Does his reverse experience strike you as real? What is said here about religious experiences?

CONSIDER PICASSO . . .

— Look at the Picasso vase-cock-hen sculpture (p. 188). What does it suggest about the roles of the sexes? What role does nature give males, especially male birds? How does this work with humanity? Think about why women go in for so much beautification in our culture. What does this suggest about the female role for us? Consider Luk's projected paper on 'The Cost of Sex and the Redundant Male' – what do you think it might involve?

CHAPTER XIII
(pp. 191–211)

Focus on: Spirit's Tigers

ASSESS AND DECIDE . . .

— Consider the make-up of the Spirit's Tigers. Think of the various personalities involved – some from psychiatric care, some from the Quakers, the Church of England, maybe the radical God-is-Dead branch. Consider also the elements of sexual greed and charisma in this group. What is the likely result of putting such elements together? Will it lead to healing, or explosion and further trauma? Who is likely to become more damaged, and who may be healed? Among this group, what are Brenda's motives? What is she likely to learn?

— If you have read *Babel Tower*, you will know Daniel's work with the 'Samaritan Group' of listeners, and will have a better idea of what made him prefer to work outside the Church. If you have also read *Still Life*, you'll know of the death of his wife Stephanie, his greatest trauma. Consider reading this particularly powerful piece of Byatt's writing, if you haven't done so already.

— What do you think of Josh Lamb's pronouncements? Could he be an example of a wise fool or holy fool?

Focus on: the image of mirrors and mirroring

LOOK OVER . . .

— There have been several episodes in the book so far where mirrors or mirror images have been used. Think over the places where you have encountered such ideas before and consider the symbolic value of mirrors and of mirroring. Why would Manichees have used them? What is the relation between Lamb's syzygos and Paul's real-life one? Why is this Other clinging to Lamb? If he could find a way of freeing himself from it, would he be able to be free, cured? What would that entail?

Focus on: healing

WONDER . . .
— Why does Gideon's approach to Lucy fail so absolutely while Lamb's approach works? Might there be an element of the sick healing the sick suggested here? But could this also be a dangerous force to play with, to send the sick among the sick of mind?

Focus on: blood

RESEARCH AND INTERPRET . . .
— Brenda seems to be rather surprised about the discussion of menstrual blood on TV (pp. 203–4). Look back at the earlier account of this episode (in Chapter IX). Do you think such things should be discussed? Why have they always been taboo in the past? Or are they still taboo? How much material is she getting for her Hen Party tapes? In fact, there is very little hen talk in this community, or Byatt gives us very little. Do you think this would be typical, or do you think she has gravitated towards the areas of sexual interest rather than female community?

Focus on: utopias

RESEARCH AND CONSIDER . . .
— The word 'utopia' derives from a fiction – *Utopia* – written in 1516 by Thomas More. This was a portrait of an ideal state, and More's invented name for his island state of Utopia was derived from the Greek. Look up 'Utopia' in a dictionary. See Dominic Baker-Smith *More's Utopia* (1991) for an excellent introduction to Thomas More and his book.

— Since Thomas More's there have been many other 'utopian' fictions, which often include some 'dystopian' features. An ideal world for one set of people may not be ideal for another group of people. Some of the best known of these fictions would include Aldous Huxley's *Brave New World* (1932), George Orwell's *Nineteen Eighty-four* (1949) and Margaret Atwood's *The Handmaid's Tale* (1985). How likely is it that the community to be based at Dun Vale Hall will 'make a good thing in this world' (p. 211)? If you have read *Babel Tower* and remember Jude's *Babbletower*, you will remember how that utopia turned out. Are utopias doomed to failure?

CHAPTER XIV
(pp. 212–22)

Focus on: Non-Maths, Anti-University

CRITICALLY EVALUATE . . .
— Consider the statement 'Reason is oppression' and evaluate it.
— Remember the incident earlier in Wijnnobel's home, and consider the remark that 'she is not his chattel'. What do you think of what she is doing, in opposition to her husband? Is he carrying altruism to absurd lengths, or not?

Focus on: Paradise

RELATE . . .
— If you look at the interview (pp. 20 and 30–31) you will see that Byatt says that she likes to end her books with a reference to John Milton's *Paradise Lost*. Here, there is the question of being closed out of Paradise. Compare this to the use of the garden myth, and closure outside it, which crops up in

Possession – Val and Roland, also Adam and Eve, the theft from Ladon, Proserpine sent down under the earth with Hades. (Byatt symbolised Stephanie as Proserpine in *The Virgin in the Garden*).

CHAPTER XV
(pp. 223–33)

Focus on: communities

LOOK OVER . . .

— Ask yourself some questions about community and the way that idealised communities might work. How important is self-sufficiency for such a community? What do you think of vegetarianism? What do you think of their attempt at 'Freeing of the Beasts of the Field'? Do you anticipate other predators might step into the freedom enabled by humanity in this case? What about closing out the outside world? Do you think there might be some dangers in this? What could they be?

Focus on: dark and light

CONNECT . . .

— Consider the names Vale of Darkness, of Tears, for Dun Vale? What does 'dun' mean? Relate this to the discussion we have heard so far about light. What do you make of the Manichee tale of the cosmos? What sense do you make of both the Kingdoms of Light and Darkness including Wind, Water and Fire? In fact, their only contrasted elements are air and light on one side, smoke and darkness on the other. If Darkness contains the principle of desire, what does light contain?

— Continue your research by focusing on the ceremony of the Solstice, and the book-burning. Research into Savonarola, but also see how many more modern book-burnings you can think of, under Islam or in China, and consider how those circumstances may help you to understand and appreciate this situation.

CHAPTER XVI
(pp. 234–63)

Focus on: images

THINK ABOUT THEME OF BLOOD . . .
— Work out the interconnections between periods, the curse, Snow White and three drops of blood. Who should Mary tell? What do you think of her anger with her mother, who 'let herself be killed by an ice-machine' and so is dropped out of her mind.

CONSIDER THE THEME OF HALF-HUMAN, HALF-BIRD . . .
— In what ways do our ideas about angels relate to half-bird, half-human creatures? Traditionally, angels are shown as male, or androgynous, rather than female, but they are also shown in female form. Compare Byatt's symbolic connections here with those in her two short stories comprising *Angels & Insects*.

LOOK FOR THE IMAGES OF HARD AND COLD . . .
— Byatt quotes from Christina Rossetti's well-known carol 'In the Bleak Mid-winter' when Mary sings it (pp. 242–3). This poem gives us the images of snow, water, ice, iron, stone. Several of these images run throughout the chapter – how many can you find and what do they suggest?

Focus on: reading

ANALYSE . . .

— Look over the discussion between Frederica and Bill about Leo's reading (p. 248). Is it surprising that a child of such a bookish family has difficulty in this area? What types of problems might be met by learners of more complex scripts, like Cyrillic Arabic, Chinese/Japanese?

Focus on: family and community

WHAT DO YOU THINK? . . .

— What does the bringing together of the community and various outsiders in this chapter add to our understanding of both?

CHAPTER XVII
(pp. 264–70)

Focus on: television

CONSIDER . . .

— In the light of the recent success of J. K Rowling's Harry Potter books, it is odd that Byatt tells us that Frederica's *Laminations* succeeds more than Agatha's *Flight North*. Do *you* find it surprising?

Focus on: allusions

RESEARCH AND ASSESS . . .

— What does 'Only Disconnect' mean? The correct quotation is 'Only connect' and is the epigraph to E. M. Forster's novel *Howards End* (1910). 'These fragments I have shored against my ruin' comes from T. S. Eliot's poem *The Waste Land* (1922).

What do these words mean for Frederica? Why does she see Diana of Ephesus in this context? Why is there no beach, shore or boat? Who is the Prince of Aquitaine and the tower? (A clue: look up the Eliot).

Focus on: censorship

DISCOVER . . .
— The next programme of *Through The Looking Glass* discusses D. H. Lawrence. Find out about the obscenity trial around *Lady Chatterley's Lover*. If you have read Lawrence's novel, consider if you believe it to be 'obscene' and how you think it is received by a contemporary audience.
— If you have read *Babel Tower*, relate this episode back to the trial and accusation of pornography brought against Jude Mason.

Focus on: the image and function of reading

ASSESS . . .
— Reading, and the power and practice of reading, are key themes for Byatt. On pp. 268–9, she quotes a passage from F. Scott Fitzgerald's *The Great Gatsby* (1925) and explains Frederica's analysis of the passage. Why do you suppose that Byatt chooses to show us this piece of teaching and learning in action? Her reaction to the reading, the hairs rising on the back of her neck, is something that she also gives us in *Possession* – when Roland and Maud find a shared line of verse from their poets, and also later when Roland rereads and understand Ash's meaning of Ash's Proserpina poem. Look for these passages and compare their significance.

CHAPTER XVIII
(pp. 271–89)

Focus on: lists

DECIDE . . .

— Consider the list of titles and speakers and decide which of them you find interesting and might wish to hear. Make a note of what kinds of purposes lists serve, and consider how lists are related to other 'ordering' tasks, such as sorting, cataloguing, filing and classifying.

Focus on: astrology

HOW MUCH DO YOU KNOW? . . .

— What do you think of Eva's interpretation of Scorpio, especially in relation to its potential for destruction? How much of yin and yang is there in the astrological system? What is the story of Selek, and Selket? What happens when 'destructiveness [is] subordinated to female wisdom and power'? (p. 288). Is this wisdom positive or negative? Think of the word Sophia, wisdom, also Athene, goddess of wisdom – wisdom is traditionally female. What is the significance of this fact? Using a dictionary of classical mythology, work out the relation between Artemis, Isis and the scorpion.

CHAPTER XIX
(pp. 290–302)

Focus on: love and desire

WHAT DO YOU THINK? . . .

— Hodgkiss offers a rather wry evaluation of his feelings of love for Potter, and his recapitulation of his love for Faber.

(Readers of *Still Life* will know that Frederica also fell in love with Faber, with rather undistinguished results.) Look over the whole of this chapter and assess the kinds of characters that desire takes in this part of the novel.

— Find out about Fibonacci. Hodgkiss tells the rather unfortunate story to Marcus at this point – but why does he tell it now and against his own good sense? Marcus indicates something in his own feelings as he says, 'The law has changed', while he moves himself very slightly away from Hodgkiss. Add this to your consideration of love and desire in this section.

CHAPTER XX
(pp. 303–18)

Focus on: narrative method

LIST AND DESCRIBE . . .
— There are several different elements contained in the narrative structure here. Write a list of each kind of narrative and add a note as to what kind it is. How does the building up of the story in this way affect your own attitude as a reader?

CHAPTER XXI
(pp. 319–30)

Focus on: symbols

THINK ABOUT AND MAKE CONNECTIONS . . .
— Frederica's programme goes on to discuss Elizabeth I. If you have read Byatt's *The Virgin in the Garden*, you will know that Frederica once played this role. Consider how this image

is used here. Consider also the discussion of 'repetition' on p. 321 and think about how this may relate to Byatt's own 'repetition' across her novels.

— Look up Andy Warhol's famous repetitive pictures of Marilyn Monroe and consider what it is that makes them art, and what the relation is between art and reproductions.

Focus on: irony

WORK OUT . . .
— Luk works on 'the redundant male' and is a peacock himself. Work out the ways that this is so. Remember these facts as they will build up to a beautiful irony later.

Focus on: metaphors

ANALYSE AND RELATE . . .
— Comment on Frederica's thoughts of herself as 'a clever metaphor' and as a 'mermaid in a raree show' (p. 326). If Frederica is a clever metaphor, what do you suppose that she means? On this page she considers her choices in life, not choosing the academic life of considering metaphor. Look back at the interview (p. 25) with Byatt and see what she has to say on the subject of metaphor there.

CHAPTER XXII
(pp. 331–45)

Focus on: twins, doubleness and wordplay

IMAGINE . . .
— Think about the Henry Moore statue (p. 331), and the image of the twins sitting in the garden. To whom does the 'they' of the second paragraph refer? What is Byatt doing with this 'they'?

Consider the possibility that it is intentionally confusing, in order to make you consider twinning and 'doubleness'.

ASK YOURSELF . . .
— Consider the play of words in 'A space for contemplation, for concentration. A concentration camp' (p. 333). What is loaded here – the words, or the culture? We can never get back to before that particular use of the word 'concentration'. Can you think of any other such word combinations which transform our understanding to give a more grave, or serious, meaning to an otherwise simple phrase?

Focus on: poetry and allusion

LOOK BACK AND FORWARD . . .
— The song of the 'One and the Many' (p. 337), like the Mickey poem, comes up later strategically. How does it relate to the Manichees' ideas? Consider and assess the image of fire in flame, crystal in cone, red thread in bone and shadow in the sun. Work out which of these are metaphors and how the language is working to suggest connections.

Focus on: characterisation

LOOK OVER AND COMPARE . . .
— Analyse the two quarrels. Look at the argument between the Wijnnobels and at Eva's ability to read his mind, claiming her rights and leaving him crestfallen. Do you feel that you are on one side or the other? If so, which? Why do you think that they stay together?
— Then look at the argument between John and Frederica. Note how the 'lowered crest' in defeat is repeated in antithesis, counterpoise, to defeat the male. Actually, we are shown inside this latter quarrel and see that Frederica is broken by her stand, at least for a time.

Focus on: symbolism

WORK OUT . . .
— On p. 341, Frederica dreams about having sex with Luk. Consider the terms of this dream and work out what this has to do with Alice's encounter with the bird.

Focus on: language

CONSIDER THE IMAGE AND THE WORDS . . .
— Can you make another sentence like 'Colourless green ideas sleep furiously' (p. 344)? What is it about this sentence that makes grammatical but not common sense? Much could change if ideas became animated, as a cartoon could make them; then you might have an oxymoronic sentence. What do you think of the image of the brain as a loom?
— 'Poetry struck out of everything like sparks from flint' (p. 344). We still use this image, although few of us ever see flint sparking any more. Think of other outdated metaphors. Or of ordinary country metaphors that most people no longer understand, such as: 'the pecking order', 'allowing free rein'. Thread back to the original observation and meaning.
— What is a dead metaphor? Why are they dead? What makes metaphors work at all? Consider the glass-box metaphor – is it new, does it work, does it illuminate your understanding?

Focus on: wordplay

WHAT DO YOU THINK? . . .
— What do you suppose Byatt is suggesting with 'looming' in the last sentence (p. 345) Is she punning? If you think so, work out how.

CHAPTER XXIII
(pp. 346–64)

Focus on: metaphors and poetry

RELATE . . .

'[Astrology] lets people think in metaphors. Make lists and categories. People enjoy that. It's beautiful in its way' (p. 350). Consider how this statement of Frederica's may relate to the themes of the book as a whole.

SET YOURSELF THE TASK . . .

— Why do we need metaphor and analogy to think? Take any one page in the book and find the metaphors, and/or analogies. Analyse how they work and to what effect.

— Then do the same with a newspaper article, a textbook, a poem, an advertisement, a speech. Would you expect to find metaphor in all of these? In what degrees of frequency or intensity?

— Which literary forms seem to you most likely to include metaphors? Here is a list to help you:

● Advertisements
● Political argument
● Football commentary
● Poetry
● News reports
● Accounts
● Novels
● Minutes of business meetings
● Shopping lists

Focus on: the image of the heart

LIST AS MANY AS YOU CAN . . .
— What do you suppose Frederica means by 'heart' (p. 355)? Look at the idea of the heart and work out how many different things it may mean and how many different images may be used to represent it.

CHAPTER XXIV
(pp. 365–82)

Focus on: reference and irony

ANALYSE AND RELATE . . .
— Frederica is called 'Cocky' (p. 378) – think about why. Think also about why this might be inappropriate. Remember to relate this moment to the title of the novel, to the discussion about bird-women, and to the consideration of the differing characters of men and women.
— Note that we are going into a scene where there is a 'bower-bird's bower'. Also remember Luk's surname. Look ahead to see what happens between Luk and Frederica.

CHAPTER XXV
(pp. 383–402)

Focus on: endings, and The Winter's Tale

PLAY WITH THE ALLUSION . . .
— Shakespeare's *The Winter's Tale* (c. 1611) runs as a theme through this chapter. If you have read the play, remind yourself of the main elements of the plot. Note how the analysis

on p. 385 says that this is 'a play about rebirth after tragedy' and that it is 'a wilful device for making comedy out of tragedy by ignoring real feelings. By ignoring the feelings of a woman shut in a vault for sixteen years who then conveniently comes back to life as a statue.' Consider the ways in which you can set these themes against those played out in *A Whistling Woman*.

Focus on: symbolism

ANALYSE . . .
— What is the symbolism of rocks, stones, trees and mirrors as they are set out across this chapter?

CHAPTER XXVI
(pp. 403–11)

Focus on: the symbolism of fire and of birds

NOTE AND LIST . . .
— Look carefully over the chapter and note all the references you can find to fire and to birds. Include the last lines of the chapter on p. 411.
— How do either of these symbols connect to the themes of the novel overall?

Focus on: plotting

PONDER . . .
— What do you make of the final lines – that if Luk had asked for some kind of exclusivity or ownership, Frederica would not have been so perturbed because the laminations were slipping (presumably into place) by fire? Remember that the programme Frederica made which included discussion of Doris Lessing's *The Golden Notebook* was called 'Free Women' – a

197

reference to a section of that book, but also a key comment on Frederica's story.

Focus on: wordplay

INVENT . . .
— 'She was full of life, and afraid' (p. 411). What do you suppose this to mean? How many meanings can you find?

CHAPTER XXVII
(pp. 412–21)

Focus on: blood

WHAT DO YOU THINK? . . .
— Frederica is worried (p. 412). Think about what is going on here and relate this moment to others you have seen in the novel.

Focus on: endings

RELATE AND CONNECT . . .
— If you look back at the interview (p. 20 and 30–31), you will see that Byatt speaks about ending her novels with references to Milton's *Paradise Lost*, a poem about the fall of humanity and angels. Read the ending of *A Whistling Woman*. Think how the poem may connect to Frederica and Luk's experience. What relation may this allusion have to Frederica's relation with Luk and his science? Why do they first shout at each other?

CONSIDER THE REFERENCES . . .
— 'The world was all before them, it seemed' (p. 421). This is an allusion to Milton's *Paradise Lost*, Book VII, L. 161: 'The world was all before them, where to choose / Their place of rest, and

Providence their guide.' 'We haven't the slightest idea what to do' . . . 'We shall think of something' (p. 421). This may allude to Margaret Mitchell's well-known 1936 novel *Gone with the Wind* (1936), in which the relationships turn out more nastily, and where Rhett Butler says to Scarlett O'Hara, 'I wish I could care what you do or where you go but I can't . . . my dear, I don't give a damn,' and where Scarlett's last thought of the novel is, 'After all, tomorrow is another day.' What does Byatt suggest by this open ending? What do you think is going to happen? And how does this ending (or not-ending) relate to the beginning of the novel and the ending of Agatha's story?

Looking over the whole novel

QUESTIONS FOR DISCUSSION OR ESSAYS

1. 'Knowing is a human pleasure' (p. 249). Discuss, in relation to the themes and events of *A Whistling Woman*.

2. List and analyse all the ways in which the title – and the epigraph – connects to the themes of the novel as a whole.

3. Trace and account for the development of Frederica's character across the novel as a whole.

4. Discuss the importance of ANY TWO of these minor characters in the novel as a whole: Jacqueline, Agatha, Leo, Eva, Josh.

5. Consider the functions of metaphor and wordplay in the novel overall.

6. Compare and contrast the ending of *Possession* with the ending of *A Whistling Woman*.

Contexts, comparisons and complementary readings

These sections suggest contextual and comparative ways of reading the three texts by Byatt. You can put your reading in a social, historical or literary context. You can make comparisons – again, social, literary or historical – with other texts or art works. Or you can choose complementary works (of whatever kind) – that is, art works, literary works, social reportage or facts which in some way illuminate the text by sidelights or interventions which you can make into a telling framework. Some of the suggested contexts are directly connected to the book, in that they will give you precise literary or social frames in which to situate the novel. In turn, these are either related to the period within which the novel is set, or to the time – now – when you are reading it. Some of these examples are designed to suggest books or other texts that may make useful sources for comparison (or for complementary purposes) when you are reading *Possession, Angels & Insects* and *A Whistling Woman*. Again, they may be related to literary or critical themes, or they may be relevant to social and cultural themes current 'then' or 'now'.

Focus on: metamorphoses

RESEARCH AND COMPARE . . .

— The idea of beings who are both man and woman, or half-bird and half-human, or half-animal and half-human is one that is popular in many fairy stories and legends, and in many different cultures. Find as many such stories as you can which reflect this subject of metamorphoses. You might look up a dictionary of classical mythology. One of the most important originating texts is the collection of stories called *Metamorphoses* written by the Roman poet Publius Ovidius Naso, known as Ovid, who lived from 43 BC – AD 17. These stories are still widely read and well known in translation.

Focus on: history and fiction

RESEARCH AND CONSIDER . . .

— In *A Whistling Woman*, there are several real historical figures mentioned as well as real people living now, such as the well-known doctor, opera director and cultural commentator Jonathan Miller, the art historian Roy Strong, and the writer Doris Lessing, whose novel *The Golden Notebook* is one of the subjects of discussion on Frederica's television programme. What is the effect of Byatt's mixing the real and the fictional in this way? Did you recognise any of the names or people? If you did recognise the 'real' elements, how did it make you feel about the contemporary issues within the novel?

Focus on: Alice in Wonderland

READ AND IMAGINE . . .

— A short quotation from Lewis Carroll's *Alice in Wonderland* is one of the epigraphs to *A Whistling Woman*. There are also several other references throughout the novel. At one point the characters discuss how the poem 'Jabberwocky' works – given that so many of the words are neologisms, or made up and invented words. Frederica's television programme is, of course, called *Through the Looking-Glass* – a reference to Lewis Carroll's sequel to *Alice's Adventures in Wonderland*. Frederica herself is described several times as looking like 'an adult Alice' in her appearances on television. Read *Alice in Wonderland* and consider how the references help to open up the playfulness of *A Whistling Woman*. Think in particular about the dream-like qualities of the scenes in *Alice*, about the parade of various different characters, about the many voices, about the way that Alice herself keeps changing and metamorphosing into other shapes.

— How many of these kinds of narrative strategies might be useful in describing not only the text of *Alice in Wonderland*, but the text of *A Whistling Woman* too?

Focus on: the community and the individual

THINK ABOUT . . .

— On p. 340 John Ottakar says, 'I work to prove the individual is nothing.' Much of the argument in *A Whistling Woman* focuses on the tensions between the needs of the individual and the requirements of living in a community. How does the novel explore these issues? This is a novel set in 1968, but published in 2002. In what ways could you read the work as one that comments on contemporary concerns in the early twenty-first century?

Reference

Selected Extracts from Critical writings

These brief extracts from critical articles on Byatt's work are designed to be used to suggest angles on the text that may be relevant to the themes of the books, their settings, their literary methods, their historical contexts, or to indicate their relevance to issues, questions or problems today.

Sometimes one critic's opinion will be entirely contradicted by another's. You might use these passages to ask yourself whether or not you agree with the writer's assessments. Or else you might take phrases from these articles to use for framing questions – for discussion, or for essays – about the texts.

None of these critical opinions are the last word. They are simply contributions to a cultural debate. As such, they should be approached with intellectual interest and intelligent assessment. But in the end, it is your own reading of a text that really counts.

Christien Franken
From *A. S. Byatt: Art, Authorship,
Creativity* (2001), p. 109
On inclusiveness, ambivalence and creativity

This book contains a critical account of the contradictory, yet highly productive ways in which Byatt's
fiction and criticism move across and in and out of
Leavisite, post-structuralist and feminist debates
about art, creativity and authorship, tracing an itin-
erary of her own. One of the main conclusions to be
drawn from my investigation is that in the case of
A. S. Byatt's work, nothing is as authentic or central
as her ambivalence. In other words, A. S. Byatt's
descriptions of male writers such as Henry Severall
and Randolph Henry Ash and female visionaries
such as Anna Severall, Christabel LaMotte, Julia and
Cassandra Corbett are of great interest, precisely
because they *are* so ambivalent. They are fictional
frameworks which allow us to think better about the
complex nature of creativity and its ambivalent relation to gender because A. S. Byatt's novels perfectly
describe where the seduction of literary genius lies.
She describes male and female characters who long
for artistic genius because of the promises it contains
for the achievement of excellence and the wholeness
of art which may act as a stronghold both against
the disorder and the dullness of reality.

Sally Shuttleworth
From 'Writing Natural History: "Morpho Eugenia"',
in Alexa Alfer and Michael J. Noble, eds,
*Essays on the Fiction of A. S. Byatt: Imagining the
Real* (2001), p. 150
On narrative complexity and multiplicity of texts

In Byatt's *Angels & Insects* the contemporary frame
has gone. The two stories continue the exploration
of the Victorian preoccupation with natural history
and the spirit world started in *Possession*, but there is
no point of reference outside the nineteenth-century
frame. Perspective here is spatial rather than tem-
poral; William Adamson's experiences in the closed
aristocratic world of Bredely Hall are set in counter-
point to his memories of the tribal rituals of the
Amazon rainforest. 'Morpho Eugenia' is characterised
by a narrative movement that homes in ever more
closely on the intricate, often tortured, discourses of
the nineteenth century. This, it seems, is storytelling
armed with the collector's box and magnifying glass,
intent on revealing, both literally and metaphorically,
what G. H. Lewes called 'that great drama which is
incessantly enacted in every drop of water, every inch
of earth'.

Impersonal narrative in 'Morpho Eugenia' gives
way to a whole sequence of further *texts*: Harald
Alabaster's interminable, circular text, where he
attempts to defeat Darwin though natural theology;
the text of Matty Crompton and Adamson's book on
ants, *The Swarming City*; Adamson's personal, ago-
nised jottings on instinct and intelligence; and
Matty's fable of insect life, 'Things Are Not What
They Seem'. The effect is extraordinarily dense, a

form of double layering of natural history. We are given not only the details of a Victorian natural history text in the study of the ants, but a natural history of the lives and beliefs of the protagonists who are alike subjected to the scrutiny of the magnifying lens. The textual form of 'Morpho Eugenia' itself mirrors that of Victorian natural history as it moves increasingly inward with a dizzying sense of detail. Natural history figures as both trope and narrative model for Byatt in this novella.

Suzanne Keen
From <i>Romances of the Archive in Contemporary British Fiction</i> (2001), pp. 52–3
On the archive, the character and subject of the quest

Despite all the sharpness of her criticism of academics, Byatt's novel rescues both modern-day characters from the sterility of their scholarly existences through a rejuvenating romance about learning. As I have suggested above, Roland and Maud discover their true and best selves by finding out the truth about Ash and LaMotte. A significant portion of the gratifying fantasy of *Possession* lies in Byatt's decision to make much of the hard evidence assessable: Roland and Maud may not find absolutely everything, but they have letters, diaries, photographs, and answers to many mysteries by the end of the novel. The representation of material traces of the past and the stories they reveal to an intellectual adventurer animates the historical element of romances of the archive. As Sabine Hotho-Jackson argues, Byatt demonstrates to her fictional researchers that 'the past is made of real myth-defying people', provoking 'a humanising re-assessment of the critics' myths' – those doxa of poststructuralism and post-modernism that at first impede love and truth-seeking ('Literary' 118). Documents, photographs, imaginative re-enactments, sections in pastiche, or subplots set in earlier periods and apprehended by magic: in some way or another a romance of the archive leads the researcher to the evidence. If the contents of the archive sometimes seem familiar to scholars, as do *Possession*'s imitative literary texts, they also can surprise . . .

The researching character may arrive at the archival text on the first or last page of the novel. There may be one key text, or many scattered clues. Romances of the archive employ literary imitation (pastiche) and description of art objects (ekphrasis) when they present documents and images in their clue-revealing specificity. Extended ekphrasis brings visual objects such as photographs and paintings to the reader's inner vision; this strategy, too, has deep roots in the Spenserian romance that underlies novelistic versions of romance. Either as embedded texts or as secondary narration framed by a present-day fictional world, pastiche enables contemporary British novelists to claim the history of English letters within their fictions (though the use of pas-tiche alone does not make a novel into a romance of the archive). *Possession*'s elaborate pastiche becomes a romance of the archive when the story details the search for and reaction to the texts through which Roland and Maud reach the Victorian story. To set the other salient limit, historical reimagining of times past may not bring the material traces of that past into the hands of a researcher; hence, Byatt's twinned novellas, *Angels and Insects* (1992), though also set in the Victorian period, cannot be considered romances of the archive. When the archival material invokes an earlier period, it may be remote or recent, a single period or a sequence of different times, rendered realistically, through quotation of documents, or in fantastic re-creation.

A. S. Byatt
From 'On Fathers', in *On Histories and Stories* (2001), pp. 12–13
On history and the novel

This first essay is about narratives of war, or about war. I became interested in this subject partly because I became interested in the slippage between personal histories and social or national histories. I began to write a novel called *The Virgin in the Garden* in the 1960s. Part of the impulse behind it was that I felt that I had now lived long enough to have lived in something I experienced as 'history', and this was a great relief to me, as I didn't want to write personal novels about the constitution of the Self, and yet as a beginning novelist I had no other subject-matter I could claim. I was born in 1936, and lived through the war and its aftermath, though hardly conscious of much of it. My novel was about what was called the new Elizabethan Age, and carried with it the ghost of the first Elizabethan Age, with its English literature of the Golden Age. Part III of the projected quartet of which that novel, with its images of history was the first, appeared only in 1996 although it was set in 1968, which meant that I was doing historical research on things I had in some sense lived through. And this sense of the edge between lived and imagined history made me in turn interested in a group of novels by young men – Graham Swift, Julian Barnes, Ian McEwan, Martin Amis – about the war they were too young to have experienced, their fathers' war. I was interested in images they had fabricated that didn't quite ring true in my experience (but I was a small child, then). I was interested in how their selection of subject-matter did and didn't coincide with that of the older generation who had lived and fought in the war, my own father's generation, Henry Green, Evelyn Waugh, Burgess, Golding. I was interested in narratives written during that historical cataclysm when its end was not known, histories without hindsight or foresight.

A. S. Byatt
From *Portraits in Fiction* (2002), pp. 1–2
On the reader's role and pictures in the imagination

Portraits in words and pictures in paint are opposites, rather than metaphors for each other. A painted portrait is an artist's record, construction, of a physical presence, with a skin of colour, a layer of strokes of the brush, or the point, or the pencil, on a flat surface. A painting exists outside time and records the time of its making. It is in an important sense arrested and superficial – the word is not used in a derogatory way. The onlooker – as we shall see

– may construct a relation in time with the painter, the sitter and the recorded face, but this is a more arbitrary, less consequential time than the end-to-end reading of a book. A portrait in a novel or a story may be a portrait of invisible things – thought processes, attractions, repulsions, subtle or violent changes in whole lives, or groups of lives. Even the description in visual language of a face or body may depend on being unseen for its force. I like to say, when talking about writing, 'Imagine a woman in a chair. Now imagine that she is about thirty and dark. Now imagine that she is plump, in a green velvet dress, with her breasts showing above a décolleté neckline. Now give her big brown eyes, long lashes and necklace of emeralds. Make the chair Gothic and put a burgundy-coloured curtain behind.' Everyone who goes through this process will have a more and more precise visual image. They will resemble each other, but, I guess, not much. Everyone sees their own woman. Put in an emotional word – 'sulky', 'voluptuous', 'gentle', 'mean' – and there will be even more variants. Writers rely on the endlessly varying visual images of individual readers and on the constructive visualising work those readers do. This is the reason, I think, why I at least am very distressed to find publishers using photographs of real, identifiable people to represent my characters on the covers of novels. It limits the readers' imaginations. And beyond that, of course, it has a blasphemous feeling – as though images are being stolen and made, stolen from the photographed, interposed into my world, graven images that are somehow illicit.

Glossary of literary terms

Abstract language Language which describes its subject in general, non-sensuous terms, perhaps describing an attribute rather than a particular person or thing – in contrast to concrete language. 'Love' is an abstract image, 'the heart' is a concrete one.

Adventure A type of narrative that recounts undertakings involving risk, danger and an uncertain outcome.

Allegory A piece of fiction that can be read on both a surface and an abstract level. In an allegory, names, places and plot development are used to deliberately structure a deeper underlying meaning beyond the 'surface' story.

Allusion A deliberate reference within one body of literature to any other work of art, cultural phenomenon or historical fact. Allusions often rely for their effect on being recognisable to the reader. Occasionally, though, the very fact that they might be expected to be *not* recognisable is part of their power. For an example of this technique, look at the opening of Tom Stoppard's play *Travesties* where several of the characters speak in foreign languages or in terms that seem – or might seem – incomprehensible.

Analogy A parallel correspondence, whereby one thing is measured or explained by means of a similar – and probably more familiar – thing.

Ballad form Originally, a song that tells a story. Literary ballads retain some song-like qualities. Ballads are usually dramatic and impersonal, with quickly sketched setting and action, and sparse dialogue. They may include literary techniques such as repetition, or repetition and variation, and question and answer.

Burlesque A satirical imitation of another work of art, often dramatic. A stronger form of parody.

Centaur A race of mythological creatures, having the upper body of a man and the lower body of a horse.

Comedy A broad term for literature designed above all to engage and amuse, and in which the portrayal of the difficulties experienced by the characters gives rise to delight, not to concern. It is divided into many different kinds of comedy. Traditionally, the events in a dramatic comedy turn out happily for the main characters.

Concrete Language which describes its subject in specific, sensuous detail, perhaps describing an individual person or thing with striking particularity – in contrast to abstract language.

Connotation The implied shades of secondary meaning of a word or symbol beyond the explicit and exact meaning (which is the denotation).

Creationism The doctrine that the world was created by God in exactly the way described in the biblical Book of Genesis, and that the theory of evolution does not satisfactorily account for the existence of life on earth.

Dead metaphor A metaphor that no longer has any impact because its resonances have become so familiar and worn. But a 'dead metaphor' can be imaginatively brought back to life. For instance, when Groucho Marx was asked, 'Are you a man or a mouse?', he replied, 'Throw me a piece of cheese and you'll find out.'

Deconstruction A mode of reading which sets out to undermine the implicit claim of any text to possess meanings that are closed and determinate. It is the 'teasing out of warring significances within a text' (Barbara Johnson), resulting in the claim that the meaning of any text is open to contradictory readings.

Denotation The primary, explicit and exact meaning of a word or symbol, such as may be found in a dictionary – or in a shopping list.

Epiphany A sudden revelation or insight into the essential nature of something, especially something previously seen as ordinary. Good examples of this kind are the stories in James Joyce's collection *Dubliners* especially in the ending of the final story 'The Dead', and certain poems of Philip Larkin such as 'An Arundel Tomb' or 'The Whitsun Weddings'.

Farce Comedy which relies on improbable and ludicrous situations, stereotyped characters, broad humour and buffoonery for its effects. Charlie Chaplin's films rely on farce.

Genre A French term for a type of literary form. Literature has been classified in numerous genres and sub-genres. For instance, drama is one genre of literature; comedy is one genre of drama; and the comedy of manners is one genre of comic drama.

Juxtapose Place side by side, usually in order to highlight similarities and, principally, differences.

Metamorphosis A transformation from one thing to another, literally or metaphorically. A butterfly's metamorphosis from grub to butterfly is literal; a drunken husband's metamorphosis from Prince Charming to pig is metaphorical.

Metaphor Any figure of speech by which one thing is explained or described by another – distinctly different – thing, without the comparison being asserted. For instance, 'the whirligig of time' is a metaphor in which 'time' is the primary subject, and 'whirligig' is the 'vehicle', an image designed to show what time is like – i.e. it brings everything back round again.

Parody An imitation of a particular author's style, literary work or literary form, applied to a lowly subject, with the intention of making the original look ridiculous. It is satirical mimicry, and a type of burlesque.

Pastiche A patchwork or imitation of sentences or words from one or more authors, 'pasted' together. If intentional, it is sometimes a form of parody, but it may also be – as in the case of Byatt's poems in *Possession* – a kind of homage.

Postmodern The movement – though never characterised as such by those who practised it – which came after modernism, and which is characterised by excessive self-consciousness, self-aware literary experimentation and fragmentation of form.

Quest A type of narrative which recounts a protagonist's search for something, and the difficulties he (it has been a traditionally male endeavour) must overcome to attain it. The 'Holy Grail' may be a precious object, a secret or an arcane truth. It is a stock narrative device of medieval romance.

Romance Medieval romance is a fictional narrative (in poetry or prose) concerning the improbable goings-on of love, adventure and the marvellous, set in a chivalric, courtly world. Later romances stressed the nostalgia for such a fictional 'past'. Nowadays, the term is sometimes applied to escapist love stories, such as those published by 'romance' imprints like Mills & Boon.

Satire The literary art of making something look ridiculous in order to make a political or socio-political point through the use of scorn, ridicule, indignation or extravagant language.

Satyr A minor Greek woodland deity. A lecherous combination of horse and goat, and a regular figure at Dionysian revels.

Slapstick Low, farcical comedy, deriving principally from physical horseplay.

Biographical outline

1936 Born 24 August in Sheffield, the daughter of John
   Frederick Drabble and Kathleen Marie Bloor.
1954–7 Read English at Newnham College, Cambridge.
1957–8 Graduate study at Bryn Mawr College, Philadelphia.
   Awarded a Fellowship by the English Speaking Union.
1958–9 Graduate study at Somerville College, Oxford.
1962–7 Taught in the extra-mural department of the
   University of London.
1964 *The Shadow of the Sun* published.
1965 *Degrees of Freedom: The Novels of Iris Murdoch* published.
1965–9 Worked as a part-time lecturer in Department of
   Liberal Studies, Central School of Art and Design,
   London.
1967 *The Game* published.
1970 *Unruly Times: Wordsworth and Coleridge in Their Time*
   published.
1972–80 Lecturer at University College, London.
1977–87 Associate of Newnham College, Cambridge.
1978 *The Virgin in the Garden* published.
1981–3 Senior Lecturer at University College, London.

1983 Elected a Fellow of the Royal Society of Literature. Left academia to become a full-time writer.

1984 Became a Fellow of University College, London.

1985 *Still Life* published.

1987 *Sugar and Other Stories* published. Awarded a D.Litt. from the University of Bradford.

1990 *Possession: A Romance* published, and awarded the Booker Prize. *Passions of the Mind: Selected Writings* published. Appointed Companion of the British Empire.

1992 *Angels & Insects* published.

1993 *The Matisse Stories* published.

1994 *The Djinn in the Nightingale's Eye* published.

1995 *Imagining Characters: Six Conversations about Women Writers* (with Ignês Sodré) published.

1996 *Babel Tower* published.

1998 *Elementals* published.

1999 *The Biographer's Tale* published. Appointed Dame of the British Empire.

2000 *On Histories and Stories: Selected Essays* published.

2001 *Portraits in Fiction* published.

2002 *A Whistling Woman* published. Film of *Possession* released.

Select bibliography

WORKS BY A. S. BYATT

The Shadow of the Sun (Chatto & Windus, London, 1964; Vintage, London, 1991)

The Game (Chatto & Windus, 1967; Vintage, 1992)

The Virgin in the Garden (Chatto & Windus, 1978; Vintage, 1994)

Still Life (Chatto & Windus 1985; Vintage, 1995)

Sugar and Other Stories (Chatto & Windus, 1987; Vintage, 1996)

Possession: A Romance (Chatto & Windus, 1990; Vintage, 1991)

Angels & Insects (Chatto & Windus, 1992; Vintage, 1995)

The Matisse Stories (Chatto & Windus, 1993; Vintage, 1994)

The Djinn in the Nightingale's Eye (Chatto & Windus, 1994; Vintage, 1995)

Babel Tower (Chatto & Windus, 1996; Vintage, 1997)

Elementals (Chatto & Windus, 1998; Vintage, 1999)

The Biographer's Tale (Chatto & Windus, London, 1999; Vintage, 2001)

A Whistling Woman (Chatto & Windus, London, 2002; Vintage, 2003)

CRITICISM

Degrees of Freedom: The Novels of Iris Murdoch (Chatto & Windus, 1964; Vintage, 1994)

Unruly Times: Wordsworth and Coleridge in Their Time (Nelson, London, 1970; Vintage, 1997)

Passions of the Mind: Selected Writings (Chatto & Windus, 1991; Vintage, 1993)

Imagining Characters: Six Conversations about Women Writers (with Ignês Sodré) (Chatto & Windus, 1995; Vintage, 1996)

On Histories and Stories: Selected Essays (Chatto & Windus, 2000; Vintage, 2001)

Portraits in Fiction (Chatto & Windus, 2001; Vintage, 2002)

OTHER NON-FICTION AND CRITICAL ARTICLES BY A. S. BYATT

'The Lyric Structure of Tennyson's Maud', in *The Major Victorian Poets Reconsidered*, Isobel Armstrong, ed. (Routledge & Kegan Paul, London, 1969), pp. 69–93.

'The Obsession with Amorphous Mankind', *Encounter* (September 1966), pp. 63–9.

'People in Paper Houses: Attitudes to "Realism" and "Experiment" in English Postwar Fiction' in *The Contemporary English Novel*, Malcolm Bradbury and Edward Arnold, eds (Stratford-upon-Avon Studies, 1979), pp. 19–41.

'Reading, Writing, Studying: Some Questions about Changing Conditions for Writers and Readers', *Critical Quarterly*, Vol. 35, part 4 (Winter 1993), pp. 3–7.

'Real People and Images', *Encounter* (February 1967), pp. 71–8.

'Wallace Stevens: Criticism, Repetition, and Creativity', *American Studies*, Vol. 12, part 3 (1978), pp. 369–75.

Iris Murdoch, in the Writers and Their Work series (Longman, Harlow, 1976).

WORKS EDITED BY A. S. BYATT

Robert Browning, *Dramatic Monologues* (Folio Society, 1990)
George Eliot, *The Mill on the Floss* (Penguin Books, London and New York, 1979)
George Eliot, *Selected Essays, Poems and Other Writings* (Penguin Books, London and New York, 1989)

PREFACES WRITTEN BY A. S. BYATT

Byatt has written Prefaces to several novels including: Elizabeth Bowen's *The House in Paris*; Willa Cather's *Death Comes to the Archbishop, A Lost Lady, My Antonia, My Mortal Enemy, O Pioneers!, The Professor's House* and *Shadow on the Rock*; Grace Paley's *Enormous Changes at the Last Minute* and *The Little Disturbances of Man*.

WEBSITE INFORMATION

If you go to the official website at www.asbyatt.com you will find that some other sources for interviews and reactions are offered to you there. They change all the time, as Byatt's readers change all the time. But some of the recent offerings include:

Leslie Ambedian, 'People I Think You "Ought" to Read', http://www.tezcat.com/~ambedian/
Robert Bray, '"The Stones I Shape Endure": Dickinsonian Pastiche in A. S. Byatt's *Possession*', http://titan.iwu.edu/~bbray/stonesrev.html (accessed 22 June 2000).
Elisabeth Bronfen, 'Fairy Stories: *The Djinn in the Nightingale's Eye*' (1995), http://www.asbyatt.com/fairy.html (accessed 12 July 2001).
Glen E. Cox, 'A. S. Byatt: *Possession*', First Impressions – Instalment Seven, July 1993, http://sf.www.lysator.liu.se/sf archive/sf-texts/FirstImpressions/fi.007.html This page

contains a review of A. S. Byatt's novel, *Possession: A Romance*.

Destination England. 'Recommended Reading', http://lang.nagoya-u.ac.jp/~matsuoka/UK-Auth-HP.html This page about England lists Byatt under the Recommended Reading List.

Stephen Dondershine, 'Color and Identity in A. S. Byatt's *Possession*' (1998), http://www.sjsu.edu/depts/jwss.old/possession/dondersh.html (accessed 28 June 2000).

Dwight Garner, 'Making the Cut'. http://www.salon1999.com/06/features/granta.html This is an article about modern writers that includes a brief mention of Byatt's work.

Index on Censorship, http://www.oneworld.net/ This page is about a liberal and politically aware censorship magazine. Byatt has contributed to the magazine.

Laura Miller, 'The author of *Possession* on the dark side of utopia, the chains of literary feminism and the albatross of sex', http://www.salon1999.com/weekly/interview960617.html (accessed 17 October 1997)

TELEVISION DOCUMENTARY
In 2002, the BBC broadcast a full-length television documentary on the work of Byatt called *Scribbling*. It was directed by Leanne Klein and Nick Godwin and produced by Jonathan Hughes and was the result of three years where the filmcrew followed Byatt in her professional and writing life to create an intimate and intelligent portrait of this intellectual writer.

CRITICAL WORKS
Alexa Alfer and Michael J. Noble, eds, *Essays on the Fiction of A. S. Byatt: Imagining the Real* (Greenwood Press, Westport, Connecticut, 2001). A collection of discerning and sophisticated essays, including two on *Possession* by Jackie Buxton (a

postmodern reading) and Jean-Louis Chevalier (on conclusion in the novel), and two on *Angels & Insects* by Sally Shuttleworth (on writing natural history in 'Morpho Eugenia') and by Michael Levenson (on theory, analogy and metamorphosis). A useful bibliography, with a list of interviews with A. S. Byatt.

Susanne Becker, 'Postmodernism's Happy Ending: *Possession!*', in Beate Neumeier ed., *Engendering Realism and Postmodernism* (Rodopi, Amsterdam, 2001), pp. 17–30. Explains the relation of the novel to Gothic conventions and how they are complicated by postmodernist theory.

Catherine Belsey, *Desire: Love Stories in Western Culture* (Blackwell, Oxford, 1994).

Malcolm Bradbury, ed., *The Novel Today: Contemporary Writers on Modern Fiction* (Fontana Press, London, 1977 and 1990).

Elisabeth Bronfen, 'Romancing Difference, Courting Coherence: A. S. Byatt's *Possession* as Postmodern Moral Fiction', in *Why Literature Matters: Theories and Functions of Literature*, Rudiger Ahrens and Laurenz Volkmann, eds (Auslistische Forschungen, Heidelberg, 1996).

Elisabeth Bronfen, 'Parmenides and the contemporary British novel', in *Literature Matters*, No. 21 (December 1996).

Nancy Chinn, '"I Am My Own Riddle" – A. S. Byatt's Christabel LaMotte, Emily Dickinson and Melusina', in *Papers on Language and Literature: A Journal for Scholars and Critics of Language and Literature*, Vol. 37, part 2 (Spring 2001), pp. 179–204. Considers the revision of the works of Emily Dickinson and Alfred Tennyson's poetry in *Possession*.

Juliet A. Dusinberre, *A. S. Byatt*, in the Women Writers Series, Janet Todd, ed. (Holmes & Meier, New York, 1983), pp. 181–95.

Monica Flegel, 'Enchanted Readings and Fairy Tale Endings in A.S. Byatt's *Possession*', *English Studies in Canada*, Vol. 24, part 4 (December 1998), pp. 413–30. On enchantments and endings.

Judith Fletcher, '*The Odyssey* Rewoven: A.S. Byatt's *Angels &*

Insects', in *Classical and Modern Literature: A Quarterly*, Vol. 19, part 3 (Spring 1999), pp. 217–31. Surveys the range of Homeric sources in Byatt's novellas.

Christien Franken, 'The Turtle and Its Adversaries: Gender Disruption in A. S. Byatt's Critical and Academic Work', in *Theme Parks, Rainforests and Sprouting Wastelands: European Essays on Theory and Performance in Contemporary British Fiction*, Richard Todd and Luisa Flora, eds (Rodopi, Amsterdam, 2000), pp. 195–214. Considers Byatt's academic and inventive relationship to poststructuralist and feminist theory.

Christien Franken, *A. S. Byatt; Art, Authorship, Creativity* (Palgrave Macmillan, Basingstoke, 2001). Offers close readings of *The Shadow of the Sun, The Game* and *Possession* under the headings of 'polyvocality', the idea of the writer of genius and as proto-feminist visionary. The final chapter on *Possession* is a sensible and accomplished account of how the book writes between the lines of traditional romance and nineteenth-century history. Includes an excellent and comprehensive bibliography which also lists A. S. Byatt's published reviews and articles.

Giuliana Giobbi, 'Sisters beware of sisters: sisterhood as a literary motif in Jane Austen, A. S. Byatt and I. Bossi Fedrigotti'. *Journal of European Studies*, xxii (1992), pp. 241–58.

Jay L. Halio, ed., *A. S. Byatt* (Gale Research Company, Detroit, 1982).

Frederick M. Holmes, *The Historical Imagination: Postmodernism and the Treatment of the Past in Contemporary British Fiction* (University of Victoria, English Literary Studies, Victoria, 1997).

Sabine Hotho, '"The Rescue of Some Stranded Ghost" – The Rewriting of Literary History in Contemporary British and German Novels', in *The Novel in Anglo-German Context: Cultural Cross-Currents and Affinities*, Susanne Stark, ed.

(Rodopi, Amsterdam, 2000), pp. 385–98. Compares Byatt's relationship to postmodernist themes with the similar topics in the work of Peter Ackroyd, Sigrid Damm and Christa Wolf.

Ann Hulbert, 'The Great Ventriloquist: A. S. Byatt's *Possession: A Romance*', in *Contemporary British Writers' Texts and Strategies*, R. E. Hosmer, Jr., ed. (Macmillan Press, London, 1993).

Suzanne Keen, *Romances of the Archive in Contemporary British Fiction* (University of Toronto Press, Toronto and London, 2001). Includes a chapter on *Possession* entitled 'Romances of the Archive: Identifying Characteristics', which carefully sets out the difference between a 'university novel' and a 'romance of the archive'; lists the constituents of the archival romance – settings, 'research' features, material traces of the past; and analyses the pleasures of reading and romance.

Kathleen Coyne Kelly, '"No – I am Out – I Am Out of My Tower and My Wits": The Lady of Shalott and A. S. Byatt's *Possession*', in *On Arthurian Women: Essays in Memory of Maureen Fries*, Bonnie Wheeler and Fiona Tollhurst, eds (Scriptorium, Dallas, Texas, 2001), pp. 283–94. Deals with the idea of 'the enclosed woman' and considers Byatt's Tennysonian sources.

Kathleen Coyne Kelly, *A. S. Byatt* (Twayne Publishers and Prentice Hall International, New York, 1996).

Olga Kenyon, *Women Novelists Today: A Survey of English Writing in the Seventies and Eighties* (The Harvester Press, Brighton, 1988).

Elisabeth Anne Leonard, '"The Burden of Intolerable Strangeness": Using C. S. Lewis to See Beyond Realism in the Fiction of A. S. Byatt', *Extrapolation*, Vol. 39, part 3 (Fall 1998), pp. 236–48.

James Lesniak, ed., *A. S. Byatt*, in the Contemporary Authors: New Revision Series, Vol. 33 (Gale Research, Detroit, 1991).

227

Alan Massie, *The Novel Today: A Critical Guide to the British Novel 1970–1989* (Longman, London, 1990).

Deborah Denenholz Morse, 'Crossing the Boundaries: The Female Artist and the Sacred Word in A. S. Byatt's *Possession*', in Regina Barreca, ed., *British Women Writing Fiction* (University of Alabama Press, Tuscaloosa, Alabama, 2000), pp. 148–74. Assesses the theme of the treatment of women writers and how the concept of the holiness of the 'word' connects to that gender specific.

Adrienne Shiffman, '"Burn What They Should Not See": The Private Journal as Public Text in A. S. Byatt's *Possession*', *Tulsa Studies in Women's Literature*, Vol. 20, part 1 (Spring 2001), pp. 93–106.

Thelma J. Shinn, '"Repossessing the Romance": A. S. Byatt', in *Women Shapeshifters: Transforming the Contemporary Novel* (Greenwood, London, 1996).

Richard Todd, *A. S. Byatt*, in the Writers and Their Work series (Northcote House, Plymouth, 1997).

Nicolas Tredell, 'A. S. Byatt in Conversation', in *PN Review*, Vol. 17, part 3 [77] (January–February 1991), pp. 24–8.

Celia M. Wallhead, *The Old, the New and the Metaphor: A Critical Study of the Novels of A. S. Byatt* (Picador, London, 1999).

Chris Walsh, 'Postmodernist Reflections: A. S. Byatt's *Possession*', in *Theme Parks, Rainforests and Sprouting Wastelands: European Essays on Theory and Performance in Contemporary British Fiction*, Richard Todd and Luisa Flora, eds (Rodopi, Amsterdam, 2000), pp. 185–94. On the uses of intertextuality in the novel and the treatment of the theme of reading and its pleasures.

Louise Yelin, 'Cultural Cartography: A. S. Byatt's *Possession* and the Politics of Victorian Studies', *The Victorian Newsletter* (Spring 1992).

The editors

Jonathan Noakes has taught English in secondary schools in Britain and Australia for fifteen years. For six years he ran A-level English studies at Eton College where he is a house-master.

Margaret Reynolds is Reader in English at Queen Mary, University of London, and the presenter of BBC Radio 4's *Adventures in Poetry*. Her publications include *The Sappho Companion*, *The Sappho History* and (with Angela Leighton) *Victorian Women Poets*.

Gillian Alban wrote her doctoral thesis on the works of A. S. Byatt and the Melusine legend.

ALSO AVAILABLE IN VINTAGE LIVING TEXTS

❏	*American Fiction*	0099445069	£5.99
❏	*Martin Amis*	0099437651	£6.99
❏	*Margaret Atwood*	009943704X	£6.99
❏	*Louis de Bernières*	0099437570	£6.99
❏	*Roddy Doyle*	0099452197	£5.99
❏	*Sebastian Faulks*	0099437562	£6.99
❏	*John Fowles*	0099460882	£5.99
❏	*Susan Hill*	0099452189	£5.99
❏	*Ian McEwan*	0099437554	£6.99
❏	*Toni Morrison*	009943766X	£6.99
❏	*Iris Murdoch*	0099452227	£5.99
❏	*Salman Rushdie*	0099437643	£6.99
❏	*Jeanette Winterson*	0099437678	£6.99

- All Vintage books are available through mail order or from your local bookshop.
- Payment may be made using Access, Visa, Mastercard, Diners Club, Switch and Amex, or cheque, eurocheque and postal order (sterling only).

❏❏❏❏❏❏❏❏❏❏❏❏❏❏❏❏

Expiry Date:_____ Signature:_____

Please allow £2.50 for post and packing for the first book and £1.00 per book thereafter.

ALL ORDERS TO:
Vintage Books, Books by Post, TBS Limited, The Book Service,
Colchester Road, Frating Green, Colchester, Essex, CO7 7DW, UK.
Telephone: (01206) 256 000
Fax: (01206) 255 914

NAME: ————————————————————————————————

ADDRESS: ——————————————————————————————

————————————————————————————————————

————————————————————————————————————

Please allow 28 days for delivery. Please tick box if you do not wish to receive any additional information.
Prices and availability subject to change without notice.   ❏